Stellar Magic

About the Author

Payam Nabarz

Persian born Payam Nabarz is a Sufi and a practicing Dervish. He is a Druid in the *Order of Bards, Ovates and Druids*, and a co-founder of its *Nemeton of the Stars* Grove. Magi Nabarz is a revivalist of the Temple of Mithras, and is working toward becoming a Hierophant in the *Fellowship of Isis*. He has also worked with the *Golden Dawn* system, Thelema, Nath Tantra, Wicca, and the Craft.

He was the founder of *Spirit of Peace*, a charitable organisation dedicated to personal inner peace and world peace via interfaith dialogue between different spiritual paths.

Magi Nabarz's writings have also appeared in numerous esoteric magazines including *Touchstone* (the Journal of the Order of Bards, Ovates, Druids), *Pagan Dawn* (the Journal of the Pagan Federation), *Stone Circle, The Little Red Book, Pentacle, White Dragon, Silver Star, Cauldron, Fezana* (Zoroastrian Journal) and the *Sufi*.

His published works include:

The Mysteries of Mithras
(The Pagan Belief That Shaped the Christian World)

Divine Comedy of Neophyte Corax and Goddess Morrigan

Mithras Reader - Volume I & 2 (editor)
(An academic and religious journal of Greek, Roman, and Persian Studies)

The Persian 'Mar Nameh' (with S.H. Taqizadeh)
(The Zoroastrian 'Book of the Snake' Omens and Calendar
& The Old Persian Calendar)

If you wish to write to the author,

Payam Nabarz;
c/o Avalonia, BM Avalonia,
London, WC1N 3XX,
England, UK

www.myspace.com/nabarz

www.stellarmagic.co.uk

"Since everything is one and the One is everything, try to love and serve all, so that you will be able to love the One (the Truth)."
- Sufi poet and Pir Dr. Javad Nurbakhsh

بُرج نامه

زبرج اسد چو مه بینی نو ما ه   تو بر آسمان کن زمانی نگاه

Published by Avalonia

BM Avalonia
London
WC1N 3XX
England, UK

www.avaloniabooks.co.uk

STELLAR MAGIC
A practical guide to the rites of the moon, planets, stars and constellations.

Copyright © Payam Nabarz 2009

ISBN-10: 1905297254
ISBN-13: 978-1905297252

First Edition, 7 July 2009
Design by Satori
Cover design by Asha Pearse

Disclaimer: This book is intended as an informational guide only. Due caution should be taken by the reader should they decide to use any of the substances suggested in some of the chapters herein. The author and publisher cannot take responsibility for any allergic reaction or any other negative results.

British Library Cataloguing in Publication Data. A catalogue record for this book is available from the British Library

All rights reserved. No part of this publication may be reproduced or utilized in any form or by any means, electronic or mechanical, including photocopying, microfilm, recording, or by any information storage and retrieval system, or used in another book, without written permission from the authors.

STELLAR MAGIC

A PRACTICAL GUIDE TO THE RITES OF THE
MOON, PLANETS, STARS AND CONSTELLATIONS

PAYAM NABARZ

PUBLISHED BY AVALONIA 2009

ACKNOWLEDGEMENTS

I would like to thank the following individuals and organisations:

Asha Pearse (www.ashapearsedesign.com) for designing the cover of this book;
My father Bijan Jan for the Persian calligraphy of the Burj Nameh, in the Moon chapter. *Pedar azizam khily mamnoon, lotf kardid;*
Alison Jones for reading of this manuscript and her tremendously helpful comments and discussions over the two years it has taken to write this book;
Akashnath for reading this manuscript and his numerous helpful discussions especially on Sefer Yetzirah;
Mogg Morgan for useful discussions on the Ursa Major constellation and use of candles in the rites; Seething, as well as his helpful comment on the Dendera Zodiac;
Glyn from Arthur's Arch (www.theshamanictable.co.uk) for the gift of the altar table featuring in some of the chapters.
Tony M for taking the Egypt photos;
Julian Dourado (www.juliandourado.co.uk) for the Kore Kosmon print;
Avalonia for proofreading, their helpful editorial comments and publishing this work;
Sharron Kraus and the *'Full Moon'* group members for the cosmic monthly lunar gatherings;
The members of the Nemeton of the Stars Grove of the Order of Bards, Ovates and Druids for taking part in performing the Stellar opening rite included in this volume;
Domus Sophiae Terrae et Sanctae Gradalis Lyceum of the Fellowship of Isis, for discussion and taking part in performing some of the rites mentioned here.

Additionally for making their resources available, I would like to thank:

Sacred Texts (www.sacred-texts.com) and The Gutenberg Project (www.gutenberg.org) for their highly useful and accessible reference works;
The U.S. Naval Observatory Library for making available the illustrations from their rare books collection, including the image used on the cover of this book which is from *Atlas céleste de Flamstéed.* (www.usno.navy.mil/library/rare/rare.html);
NASA, ESA, M. Robberto (Space Telescope Science Institute/ESA) and the Hubble Space Telescope Orion Treasury Project Team for the image of Orion used on the inside title page.

Table of Contents

Acknowledgements   6

Introduction **11**
    How To Use This Manual   23

Opening & Closing Rites **29**
    Introduction   29
    Standard Opening   35
    Standard Closing   40

The Constellation Orion: Horus **43**
    Introduction   43
    Orion-Horus rite   50

Star Sirius: Sothis & Tishtrya (Tir) **59**
    Introduction   59
    Sirius Rite   62

Constellations Perseus & Andromeda **72**
    Introduction   72
    Perseus and Andromeda Rite   74

The Moon **81**
    Introduction   81
    Persian Burj Nameh: 87
    book of omens from the moon   87
    Persian calligraphy text of   89
    Burj Nameh   89
    A Rite to the Moon   92

Seven planets **100**
    Introduction   100
    Rite of the Seven Planets   102

Cygnus: Northern Cross **111**
    Introduction   111
    Astral Tour of Oxon (part I- III)   116
    Cygnus Rite   124

The Pleiades: The Seven Sisters **131**
    Introduction   131
    Pleiades Rite   134

Great Bear & Little Bear **141**
    Introduction   141
    Great Bear Rite   148

Draco **155**
    Introduction   155
    Draco rite   161

Twelve signs of the Zodiac **165**
    Introduction   165
    A Rite to the Zodiac   169

Aurora **178**
    Introduction   178
    Aurora Rite   181

The Stellar World Cave **186**
    Introduction   186
    Rite of the Stellar World Cave   190

Epilogue: Monad **198**

Bibliography **199**
    and Further reading: 200

Index **207**

"Ex Uno Omnia"
"From the One, All"

(MOTTO OF ELIAS ASHMOLE)

"The all who is one and the one who is all. For plenitude of all things is one and is in one, not because the one duplicates itself but because both are one."
> - *Hermetica,* trans Brian P. Copenhaver

INTRODUCTION

"To the Stars.

*With holy voice I call the stars on high,
Pure sacred lights and genii of the sky.
Celestial stars, the progeny of Night,
In whirling circles beaming far your light,
Refulgent rays around the heavens ye throw,
Eternal fires, the source of all below.
With flames significant of Fate ye shine,
And aptly rule for men a path divine.
In seven bright zones ye run with wandering flames,
And heaven and earth compose your lucid frames:
With course unwearied, pure and fiery bright
Forever shining thro' the veil of Night.
Hail twinkling, joyful, ever wakeful fires!
Propitious shine on all my just desires;
These sacred rites regard with conscious rays,
And end our works devoted to your praise."*

Hymns of Orpheus [1]

In Plato's *Timaeus* the view of the Planets and heavenly bodies containing gods is discussed as the necessary force that moves the planets around the earth. The Greek cosmology viewed the movement of celestial bodies to be *"resembling as closely as possible the perfect intelligible Living Creature."* The laws of Newtonian physics have long ago replaced the need for gods as the necessary force for movement of stellar bodies, thus astronomy has taken over from astrology.

Yet, when walking on a clear night and staring at the stars, something does capture one's imagination. It may be the simple beauty of the stars and the planets, or perhaps a religious meme that compels one to head out night after night in the footsteps of the modern and ancient stargazers. It is not only the full moon that turns people into lunatics and poets; there are other subtle forces there too that inspire us; the constellations. To use a metaphor, if the sun is the ocean and the moon a sea, the planets the rivers, then the constellations are the streams. There has been much written about the magic of the sun, moon and the planets, yet the gentler streams of the constellations remain largely unspoken of. The constellations that are popular are the twelve signs of the Zodiac, which are seen as part of the celestial powers that influence us from birth. However, in modern astrology the interaction with the constellations is a reactive rather proactive relationship viewed as a unidirectional flow of energy from the heavens to us; this is referred to as *'divinatory astrology'* by the Swiss mystical writer Titus Burckhardt in his book *Mystical Astrology according to Ibn Arabi*[2]. The field of divinatory astrology is well covered by thousands of books on the subject and it is part of popular culture, with many newspapers printing daily horoscopes. Divinatory astrology is a practice which goes back centuries, for example in the Persian *Shah Nameh* (Epic of Kings) circa 1000 AD we read:

> " When Feridoun had thus opened his lips he called for the book wherein are written the stars, and he searched for the planets of his sons. And he found that Jupiter reigned in the sign of the Archer in the house of Silim, and the sun in the Lion in that of Tur, but in the house of Irij there reigned the moon in the Scorpion. And when he saw this he was sorrowful, for he knew that for Irij were grief and bale held in store. Then having read the secrets of Fate, Feridoun parted the world and gave the three parts unto his sons."[3]

Another example is the well known testing of astrologers by Roman Emperor Tiberius (42 BC – 37 AD), his method of testing was:

> "Whenever he (Emperor Tiberius) sought counsel on such (astrological) matters, he would make use of the top of the house and of the confidence of one freedman, quite illiterate and of great physical strength. The man always walked in front of the person whose (astrological) science Tiberius had determined to test, through an unfrequented and precipitous path (for the house stood on rocks), and then, if any suspicion had arisen of imposture or of trickery, he hurled the astrologer, as he returned, into the sea beneath, that no one might live to betray the secret. (Astrologer) Thrasyllus accordingly was led up the same cliffs, and when he had deeply impressed his questioner by cleverly revealing his imperial destiny and future career, he was asked whether he had also thoroughly ascertained his own horoscope, and the character of that particular year and day. After surveying the positions and relative distances of the stars, he first paused, then trembled, and the longer he gazed, the more was he agitated by amazement and terror, till at last he exclaimed that a perilous and well-nigh fatal crisis impended over him. Tiberius then embraced him and congratulated him on foreseeing his dangers and on being quite safe. Taking what he had said as an oracle, he retained him in the number of his intimate friends." - 6.21 The Annals by Publius Cornelius Tacitus.[4]

However, the focus of the work in this book is on divinatory astrology's less popular cousin, which Titus Burckhardt refers to as *'spiritual astrology'*. The aims of following stellar workings are to make such relationships a bidirectional flow of energy and to honour the constellations in the same way many modern Pagans honour the earth, the moon, the sun and the planets. To draw down the powers of the constellations as some modern Pagans draw down the moon or the sun, or as some magicians work with planetary hours and days of the week for the ideal time in which to achieve their aims or create talismans as we see in works like the *Picatrix* or *The Key of Solomon.*

In following the approach of using star lore for spiritual astrology and not just divinatory purposes, we are in good company as this is in line with the *Chaldean Oracles*:

> *"Theurgists fall not so as to be ranked among the herd that are in subjection to Fate. The Oracles also tell us: 'Direct not thy mind to the vast surfaces of the Earth; for the Plant of Truth grows not upon the ground. Nor measure the motions of the Sun, collecting rules, for he is carried by the Eternal Will of the Father, and not for your sake alone. Dismiss (from your mind) the impetuous course of the Moon, for she moves always by the power of necessity. The progression of the Stars was not generated for your sake. The wide aerial flight of birds gives no true knowledge nor the dissection of the entrails of victims; they are all mere toys, the basis of mercenary fraud; flee from these if you would enter the sacred paradise of piety, where Virtue, Wisdom and Equity are assembled.'"*[5]

The point is succinctly made by W.W. Westcott in his introduction to the *Chaldean Oracles*:

> *"Although destiny, our destiny, may be 'written in the Stars' yet it was the mission of the divine Soul to raise the human Soul above the circle of necessity, and the Oracles give Victory to that Masterly Will, which:*
> *'Hews the wall with might of magic,*
> *Breaks the palisade in pieces,*
> *Hews to atoms seven pickets . . .*
> *Speaks the Master words of knowledge!'*
> *The means taken to that consummation consisted in the training of the Will and the elevation, of the imagination, a divine power which controls consciousness."*[6]

In other words, an initiate has to exceed the total sum of their programming, and using their spiritual training, go beyond the boundaries set at the time of birth, be they social, intellectual, physical, astrological, or religious boundaries. An initiate at all times aspires consciously to improve themselves, for example, as Sufis aim to become an *'Insan Kamil'* (a perfect or complete human). An intellectual study of the occult and mysticism on its own is not enough; let us look at magical arts and witchcraft. The word art is important here, magic can be an art like any other art; witch-craft is a craft like any other craft. When someone practices an art or craft, be it painting, academic research, music, gardening or sport etc... they are all going on similar skill journey to their fellow magical arts practitioners. It is the journey, the trials, approbations, and continuous overcoming of obstacles and pushing oneself to improve that makes the difference and can result in making contact with your divine spark, the higher self or according to Greek philosophy your Daimon or the Holy Guardian Angels in Christian and Zoroastrian religions. The rough Ashlar stone becomes smooth or the grape turns to the Sufi's wine of ecstasy; the cosmic transformation and metamorphosis. What is interesting is when someone masters their art or craft or sport; their piece of music, or performance, or spell or rite, or painting etc. This transforms them, and also influences others in a major way too.

The *Chaldean Oracles* encourage us to:

"Explore the River of the Soul, whence, or in what order you have come: so that although you have become a servant to the body, you may again rise to the Order from which you descended, joining works to sacred reason....Every way unto the emancipated Soul extend the rays of Fire......Let the immortal depth of your Soul lead you, but earnestly raise your eyes upwards...... Who knoweth himself, knoweth all things in himself."

This is a highly significant text which draws upon Neo-Platonism and other teachings; therefore the whole text of the *Chaldean Oracles* is part of the recommended reading and bibliography, which is detailed at the end of this book.

This magical and religious approach to the constellations is not a new idea; indeed it can be viewed as the root of many ancient religions. Prof Franz Cumont in his *Astrology and Religion among the Greeks and Romans* raises the issue of *"the idea that the primary source of religion was the spectacle of celestial phenomena and the ascertainment of their correspondence with earthly events, and he (Dupuis) undertook to show that the myths of all peoples and all times were nothing but a set of astronomical combinations."*[7] The field of archaeoastronomy has shown us numerous religious structures since the Megalithic had cosmological roles and were aligned to the stars, moon or the sun. Examples from that period include Callanish in Scotland, Stonehenge in England, the Pyramids of Giza in Egypt, and Newgrange in Ireland.

The central role of the stars in the root of religions is also echoed in our time in a myriad of manifestations; from Star Gate fans, to UFO enthusiasts, to fanatical Solar Temple cult followers. From the ancient stargazers to modern astronomers and New Age astrologers the stars still inspire - the thoughts of the Magi still resonate today.

The place of stellar magic in modern occultism is best seen in the works of Rudolf Steiner and Aleister Crowley. Aleister Crowley talks of the Star Goddess Nuit in his *Book of the Law (Liber AL vel Legis)* in depth, indeed the first chapter of this book is of Nuit speaking directly to the reader; for example, she states: *"I am the blue-lidded daughter of Sunset; I am the naked brilliance of the voluptuous night-sky."* and *"Had! The manifestation of Nuit, The unveiling of the company of heaven, Every man and every woman is a star."*

He also refers to Nuit in a number of his other works, for example:

"It is written in The Book of the Law: Every man and every woman is a Star. It is Our Lady of the Stars that speaketh to thee, O thou that art a star, a member of the Body of Nuith! Listen, for thine ears become dulled to the mean noises of the earth; the infinite silence of the Stars woos thee with subtle musick... For inasmuch as thou hast made the Law of Freedom thine, as thou hast lived in Light and Liberty and Love, thou hast become a Free-man of the City of the Stars..."- Liber CVI.[8]

Rudolf Steiner, the founder of the Anthroposophical Society, also developed a stellar based approach philosophy, and, in 1913 built the first Goetheanum, a physical temple so to speak, to connect to the stars. In his words:

"The stars once spoke to man.
It is world destiny that they are silent now
To become aware of this silence can be pain for earth humanity
But in the deepening silence
There grows and ripens what human beings speak to the stars
To become aware of this speaking
Can become strength for Spirit Man."

In his view, the stellar connection was a crucial step in one's spiritual journey:

"Steiner explained that to know the human being, one must take ... the heavens and the earth as your province and discern the rhythm that beats between them."[9]

My own interest in theurgy and stellar magic is rooted in the Mithraic Mysteries. In this stellar religion, the individual's soul is seen to have descended from the starry heavens to earth and at death the soul makes its journey upwards again into the firmament, a vision similar to the Biblical vision of Jacob's ladder. The initiatory system allowed the neophyte to become familiar with the cosmos, and learn the star *'signposts'* which would have allowed his return journey to be smoother and reach a state of henosis (union with the divine, the source). The cave-like temple, (called a Mithraeum) was a representation of the universe; here the initiate ascended through various planetary degrees and learned about the constellations and their meanings. The Mithraeum is an authentic microcosm, literally a model of the heavens. Prof. Roger Beck describes the Mithraeum as an *'image of universe'*. The Planetary initiates were:

- ⊕ Mercury (Corax/Raven)
- ⊕ Venus (Nymphus/bee chrysalis or male bride)
- ⊕ Mars (Miles/soldier)
- ⊕ Jupiter (Leo/lion)
- ⊕ Moon (Perses/Persian)
- ⊕ Sun (Heliosdromus)
- ⊕ Saturn (Pater)

According to Porphyry, *On the Cave of the Nymphs*:
> "Thus also the Persians, mystically signifying the descent of the soul into the sublunary regions, and its regression from it, initiate the mystic (or him who is admitted to the arcane sacred rites) in a place which they denominate a cavern. For, as Eubulus says, Zoroaster was the first who consecrated in the neighbouring mountains of Persia, a spontaneously produced cave, florid, and having fountains, in honour of Mithra, the maker and father of all things; a cave, according to Zoroaster, bearing a resemblance of the world, which was fabricated by Mithra. But the things contained in the cavern being arranged according to commensurate intervals, were symbols of the mundane elements and climates."[10]

The central iconography of Mithraism (For full details see *The Mysteries of Mithras: The Pagan Belief That Shaped the Christian World* by Payam Nabarz) is called *'Tauroctony'* or the Bull Slaying; this was a representation of the night sky and structure of the Mithraeum building lends itself to contain all the symbols of the macrocosm. The scene shows that Mithras, while facing away from the bull, has one leg on the back of the bull, one hand holding the bull's head, and the other hand stabbing the bull in the neck, where blood pours forth. Around him are a dog, a raven, a scorpion, a snake, a lion, and a cup. From the tip of the bull's tail, a shaft of wheat is growing. The cloak of Mithras is the night sky with stars; the signs of the zodiac surround the whole scene. The symbols of the seven planets are present; the two torchbearers of Mithras stand at either side of the bull-slaying scene. One of the Mithraic mysteries is that the bull slaying scene is a representation of the constellations Perseus (Mithras), Taurus (bull), Canis Minor (dog), Hydra (snake), Corvus (raven), and Scorpio (scorpion). The wheat is the star Spica (the brightest star in the constellation Virgo); where the knife enters the bull, it is the Pleiades; the life giving blood of the bull is the Milky Way. The two torchbearers, Cautes and Cautopates, symbolise the equinoxes. Cautes' torch is pointing upward: the spring equinox. Cautopates' torch is pointing downward: the autumn equinox.

MITHRAS SLAYING THE BULL. ROTATING DOUBLE-FACED ALTAR PANEL, SIDE A. MUSÉE DU LOUVRE, PARIS. (PHOTOGRAPH BY P. NABARZ WITH KIND PERMISSION OF THE MUSEUM)

Several key images around the central Tauroctony scene are important because they contain a creation story. In the beginning Mithras is asked by the Sun to kill the first bull, but he is reluctant to do this. The Raven, the messenger of the Sun, comes to him again with the message. Mithras goes into the field and captures the bull, and with his might, lifts the back legs of the bull over his shoulder and drags him to the birth cave. The crescent moon over the bull suggests its connection to the moon. As Mithras kills the bull, from his blood come wine and all the plants that cover the earth. The tail becomes wheat, which gives us our bread. The seed and the genitals of the bull are taken to the Moon Goddess and purified, giving rise to all the animals. Hence, by this slaying of the first bull, life comes onto the earth. The new life on Earth is growing very slowly, due to drought. Mithras as the mediator between Heaven and Earth is asked to solve this problem; however, this means a conflict with the Sun, who has been burning the land. The battle between Sol (the sun) and Mithras results in Mithras overcoming the planetary sun and becoming the Invincible Sun. Sol kneels in front of Sol Invictus while Mithras holds the constellation the Great Bear in one hand. This emphasizes his power as the stellar god, one who moves the cosmic pole as well as causing the precession of equinoxes. Mithras and Sol then become friends and shake hands with their right hands. Mithras is referred to *kosmokrator* (ruler of cosmos) and also rules the movements of the earth and the seasons as his number is 365, number of days in a year.

THE SEVEN GRADES OF INITIATION, MITHRAEUM OF FELISSIMUS, OSTIA ITALY, PHOTO BY P. NABARZ

The emblems for the first Grade, the Corax, appear toward the bottom of the left photo and the grades proceed upward in order to

Grade seven, the Pater, at the top of the right photo. The emblems, or tokens, for each grade are shown as follows. The tokens of Corax under the planet Mercury are: a Raven, a Caduceus, and a small beaker. The tokens of Nymphus under Venus are: an oil lamp and a diadem. The tokens of Miles under Mars are: a lance, a helmet, and a soldier's sling bag. The tokens of Leo under Jupiter are: a fire shovel, a rattle (sistrum), and a thunderbolt. The tokens of Perses under the Moon are: a sickle, a Persian dagger, and a crescent moon with a star. The tokens of Heliosdromus under the Sun are: a torch, a seven-rayed crown, and a whip. The tokens of the Pater under Saturn are: a Phrygian cap, a libation bowl, a staff, and a sickle.

In making their Hermetic ascent, the Mithraic initiates were magical cosmonauts, making astral journeys and making preparations for their final destination; returning to the Milky Way. The Neoplatonic based ideals allows the ascent of the soul through the planetary spheres, an initiatory voyage to purify the divine aspects hidden in mankind from its contact with matter from birth. For further details of Mithraic cosmic soul travellers and star talk, see *The Religion of the Mithras Cult in the Roman Empire: Mysteries of the Unconquered Sun* by Roger Beck.

The following rites are experimental and designed to help to increase our knowledge of the stars, to learn about their myths and finally to allow connection to these stellar bodies and revelation of their mysteries to each person in their own way.

This is indeed the basis of Aleister Crowley's saying *'Every Man and Woman is a Star'*, and we all aim for our one star in sight; a view that we have inherited from the Ancient Greeks, as we see in Plato's *Timaeus*:

> *"Thus he spoke, and once more into the cup in which he had previously mingled the soul of the universe he poured the remains of the elements, and mingled them in much the same manner; they were not, however, pure as before, but diluted to the second and third degree. And having made it he divided the whole mixture into souls equal in number to the stars, and assigned each soul to a star; and having there placed them as in a chariot, he showed them the nature of the universe, and declared to them the laws of destiny, according to which their first birth would be one and the same for all,-no one should suffer a disadvantage at his hands; they were to be sown in the instruments of time severally adapted to them, and to come forth the most religious of animals; and as human nature was of two kinds, the superior race would here after be called man. Now, when they should be implanted in bodies by necessity, and be always gaining or losing some part of their bodily substance, then in the first place it would be necessary that*

they should all have in them one and the same faculty of sensation, arising out of irresistible impressions; in the second place, they must have love, in which pleasure and pain mingle; also fear and anger, and the feelings which are akin or opposite to them; if they conquered these they would live righteously, and if they were conquered by them, unrighteously. He who lived well during his appointed time was to return and dwell in his native star, and there he would have a blessed and congenial existence."[11]

According to the classical writers it is not only the human souls that originate in the stars and strive to return to them. The gods too have their origins among the stars, in the *Hermetica* (the Greek *Corpus Hermeticum*) we read about the birth of the universe and life and a creation story which is centred on the stars:

"In the deep there was boundless darkness and water and fine intelligent spirit, all existing by divine power in chaos. Then a holy light was sent forth, and elements solidified out of liquid essence. And all the gods (divide the parts) of germinal nature. While all was unlimited and unformed, light elements were set apart to the heights and the heavy were grounded in the moist sand, the whole of them delimited by fire and raised aloft, to be carried by spirit. The heavens appeared in seven circles, the gods became visible in the shapes of the stars and all their constellations, and the arrangements of (this lighter substance) corresponded to the gods contained in it. The periphery rotated (in) the air, carried in a circular course by divine spirit."[12]

The scope of this book does not extend to the whole of the 88 modern constellations, it only covers some of the main constellations from the 48 classical constellations as seen in works such as Ptolemy's *The Almagest* (circa 150 AD), Aratus' *Phaenomena* (275 BC), Eratosthenes' *Constellations* (1st/2nd century AD), and Hyginus' *De Astronomia* (1st century BC).[13, 14] These are the most ancient known constellations that are mentioned in the Babylonian *A Prayer to Gods of the Night* (circa 1700 BC) and Mul.APIN tablets (600 BC) where the origin of our modern constellation is rooted. [13-20]

The practical nocturnal rites and ceremonies here are created using a myriad of hymns and tales, drawing inspiration and material from many ancient, classical and medieval sources including: the *Hymns of Orpheus*, Ovid's *Metamorphoses*, Plato's *Timaeus*, the *Hermetica*: the Greek *Corpus Hermeticum* and the Latin *Asclepius*, the *Greek Magical Papyri*, the *Chaldean Oracles*, the Persian *Shah Nameh 'Epic of Kings'* by Ferdowsi, *Scipio's Dream* by Cicero, the Persian *Pahlavi Texts*, the *Book of Enoch*, the *Book of Ezekiel*, Egyptian temples and texts, *The Golden Ass* by Lucius Apuleius, the

Zoroastrian Yasht hymns, Sufi works of Ibn Arabi and Rumi, the Kabbalistic *Sefer Yetzirah*, the *Mithras Liturgy,* Persian *Burj Nameh*, Hesiod *Works and Days,* Homer's *The Odyssey,* Porphyry's *On the Cave of the Nymphs* and Aratus' *Phaenomena.*

In bringing these ancient rites into modern times, stellar related material and ideals by modern poets such as WB Yeats, Robert Graves, Sylvia Plath, and esoteric writers such as John Milton, John Dee, Elias Ashmole, Francis Barrett, Rudolf Steiner, Aleister Crowley, Gerald Gardner have also been included, giving a Bardic blend of the ancient and the modern. The rites here *'set the scene'* and after all the poems and invocations are uttered, the point is reached in the rite where the magus has to make his/her direct connection, and to draw inspiration from the stellar well directly. The rites here are the beginning steps on your stellar journey, it is recommended that you write your own poems and invocations to the constellations and make your Path to the stars.

This is a highly accessible, succinct and practical book on this complex subject. It is written in such a way that it can be used as a manual and workbook for practising stellar magic or simply to read for gaining insight into star lore.

References
1. *The Hymns of Orpheus* translated by Thomas Taylor, 1792.
2. *Mystical Astrology According to Ibn Arabi* by Titus Burckhardt, Beshara Publications, 1977.
3. *The Epic of Kings* by Ferdowsi Translated by Helen Zimmern, 1883.
4. *6.21 The Annals* by Publius Cornelius Tacitus. Translated by Alfred John Church and William Jackson Brodribb, *The Complete Works of Tacitus*, 1942.
5. *The Chaldean Oracles Attributed to Zoroaster. Edited and revised* by W.W. Westcott, 1895, pp45-46. Sure Fire Press, Edition 1984.
6. *The Chaldean Oracles Attributed to Zoroaster* by W.W. Westcott, 1895, p21. Sure Fire Press, Edition 1984.
7. *Astrology and Religion Among the Greeks and Romans*, Franz Cumont, 1912.
8. *Liber CVI,* Aleister Crowley.
9. *Speaking to the Stars: In consideration of Cosmic Ritual* by Mary Stewart Adams in New View Winter 2006/7 p50.
10. *On the Cave of the Nymphs* in the Thirteenth Book of the Odyssey from the Greek of Porphyry translated by Thomas Taylor, 1823.
11. *Timaeus* By Plato Written 360 B.C.E Translated by Benjamin Jowett. New York, C. Scribner's Sons, 1871.

12. *Hermetica*: The Greek *Corpus Hermeticum* and the Latin Asclepius in a New English Translation, with Notes and Introduction by Brian P. Copenhaver, 1992, p13.

13. *The Origin of the Greek Constellations*, Schaefer, Bradley E, Scientific American, Nov 2006, pp70-75.

14. *Star Myths of the Greeks and Romans: A Sourcebook* by Theony Condos. Phanes Press, U.S. Nov 1997.

15. *Another Old Babylonian Prayer to the Gods of the Night*, Horowitz, Wayne and Wasserman, Nathan; 1996; in *Journal of Cuneiform Studies*, Vol. 48:57-60.

16. *Babylonian Astrological Omens and Their Stars*, Lambert, W.G., *Journal of the American Oriental Society*, Vol. 107, No. 1 (Jan. - Mar., 1987), pp. 93-96.

17. *Astral Magic in Babylonia*, Reiner, Erica; 1995; in *Transactions of the American Philosophical Society*, New Series, Vol. 85.4:i-150.

18. *Some of the Sources of the Ghāyat al-hakīm*, Pingree, David; 1980; in *Journal of the Warburg and Courtauld Institutes*, Vol. 43:1-15.

19. *The Uses of Astrology*, Reiner, Erica; 1985; in *Journal of the American Oriental Society*, Vol. 105.4:589-95.

20. *Ascent to the Stars in a Mesopotamian Ritual*, Abusch, Tzvi, in *Death, Ecstasy, and Other Worldly Journeys*, edited by John J. Collins and Michael Fishbane, Albany, NY. State University of New York Press. 1995. pp. 18-23.

How To Use This Manual

"The function of ritual, as I understand it, is to give form to human life, not in the way of mere surface arrangement, but in depth."

– Joseph Campbell, *Myths to live by*.

This is a beginner's book and as such it is hoped this book will be a platform upon which the reader will build their own more complex magical ideas and rites. The practitioner is highly encouraged to develop their own rites, style and content and not purely subscribe to material provided here without personal thought. The words of William Blake should always be borne in mind, as he said: *"I must create my own system or be enslaved by another man's."*

Some practical pointers in using this manual are that these are nocturnal rites, and, if performed outside, appropriate outdoor clothing should be worn and adequate preparation should be undertaken. A pair of binoculars or a telescope will also be useful for looking at the stars before starting the rites. Using a small focused light torch or a red light torch would be best for reading the texts in the dark, as this means one's night vision will not be impaired when also looking at the stars.

An intrinsic part of this approach is the steps that will convert this book from a body of mass produced identical books, to a working magical Grimoire; thus creating a working personal version for each practitioner. To transform the book into a working Grimoire; the practitioner is required to put their own energy into it in the form of reworking some of the text in their own handwriting. This is a simple technique which will make each copy unique to each practitioner. For this purpose there are blank pages with the heading 'Notes' at the end of each rite.

For example, there are a number of poems or hymns where only a few lines are mentioned. In order to engage with these, the practitioner needs to read from the original texts which are referred to. For ease of locating the full texts, both the online links and textual source details are provided.

If using poems, liturgies, hymns and invocations is not your preferred method, then creating your own chants and sigils based on the material is recommended. At end of each chapter there are some blank pages for making your own notes. All of these rites are written as group ceremonies, with different people performing different roles, though the rites can be altered to fit solo workings also. The format of many of the rites here is along the lines of a Bardic *Eisteddfod*, in which great poems are recited. In the case of some of the rites the hymns, poems, liturgies or invocations are several pages long, which might be difficult to memorise and recite; therefore the practitioner should read them out from the book. The reason several invocations are included is that if the Bards approach to magic and the *Eisteddfod* format does not appeal to a reader, then they can choose the one invocation that appeals to them most, and/or create an abridged version of the rite, in which it can be performed from memory and without any reference to books or printed material. In addition, having several hymns, poems and invocations included allows readers who are not using the book as a magical workbook to still read it and learn about star lore.

Following in the footsteps of the old Persian Magi, the book here has taken four years to write and is the summary of my study and practise working toward my Heirophancy within the Fellowship of Isis as well as my other Mithraic and Druid work. This period included my role in co-founding with two other Druids the *'Nemeton of Stars'* Grove within the Order of Bards, Ovate and Druids. The Stellar rites here are influenced by the Bardic current, and *Eisteddfod* format hence the use of numerous liturgies and poems.

There are a number of software programs available which can help with familiarizing oneself with the night sky, for example http://earth.google.com and www.stellarium.org.

It is useful to buy yourself a Planisphere and a Star Globe, also it may be a good idea to read a monthly astronomy magazine such as *The Sky at Night*.

If the ceremonies are performed indoors, a home planetarium or star theatre could be projected onto a ceiling and music could be played; relevant music could help in setting the scene. For example, if working with the planets the CD *'Secrets of the Heavens'* which contains seven planetary invocations (performed in the spirit of Orphic singing of the 15th century philosopher Marsilio Ficino), or Gustav Holst's *Planets* Suite is a good choice. Other music such as Sufi singing, Hindu chanting, or any other music which you find inspiring could help to create a productive and creative atmosphere.

Once you have performed all the rites here and are familiar with the myths, legends and current of the constellations; then your experience of walking on a clear night is no longer akin to observing a *'star chart'* of dots connected with lines. Now looking at the night sky is like watching a motion picture, and, feels more akin to looking at a family album, filled with emotions, living stories and deep connections.

> *"We are stardust, we are golden,*
> *We are billion year old carbon."*
> - Crosby Stills Nash & Young

Online

To support the work in this book and allow discussion with others practising the material, I have set up several online community groups. All readers are welcome to join. Furthermore, many of the images and photos in this book are in colour, although it is printed in black and white; the colour images are available in the community and can be accessed there.

To subscribe to the Stellar Magic book discussion groups:

Yahoo eGroup:
Yahoo: http://groups.yahoo.com/group/StellarMagic

Facebook Discussion Group:
www.facebook.com/groups/edit.php?customize&gid=18128039869#/group.php?gid=18128039869

MySpace Group:
http://groups.myspace.com/index.cfm?fuseaction=groups.groupProfile&groupID=107460838

Stellar Magic Tribe:
http://tribes.tribe.net/stellarmagic

Stellar Magic Website:
For website of this book, resources and updates see: www.stellarmagic.co.uk

Additional Material

To ensure you receive the maximum benefits from the material in this book, I would recommend you look up the *Star-Talk* poem by Robert Graves (1895 - 1985). It is from *The Complete Poems (Poetry Pleiade: the Millennium Graves* from Carcanet Press, 2000), the poem can be found on page 4.

Additionally it will enhance your appreciation of the material if you look up any of the sources given subsequently below the

Babylonian *A Prayer to Gods of the Night* (circa 1700 BC). The prayer starts: *"May the great gods of the night: shining Fire-star (Sirius), heroic Irra (Mars)..."* and the translation is that of Oppenheim, *Analecta Biblica* 12 (1959) 295f, with some modifications and some modern names added.

Here is my own simpler version based on the above translation.

> *"Great gods of the night,*
> *bright flaming Sirius,*
> *great warrior Mars*
> *Bow star and Bootes*
> *Pleiades, Orion and Draco,*
> *Great Bear, and Lyra,*
> *Bison star and the Serpent,*
> *heed my words and give thy aid in my operation."*

The practitioner is encouraged to personalise the other prayers and poems in the rites in a similar way.

For further information on *A Prayer to Gods of the Night* prayer see:

Another Old Babylonian Prayer to the Gods of the Night, by Wayne Horowitz, and Nathan Wasserman, which can be found in the *Journal of Cuneiform Studies,* Vol. 48:57-60 (1996);

Babylonian Astrological Omens and Their Stars, by W.G. Lambert; 1987; in the *Journal of the American Oriental Society,* Vol. 107.1:93-6,

Astral Magic in Babylonia, by Erica Reiner; 1995; in *Transactions of the American Philosophical Society,* New Series, Vol. 85.4:i-150.

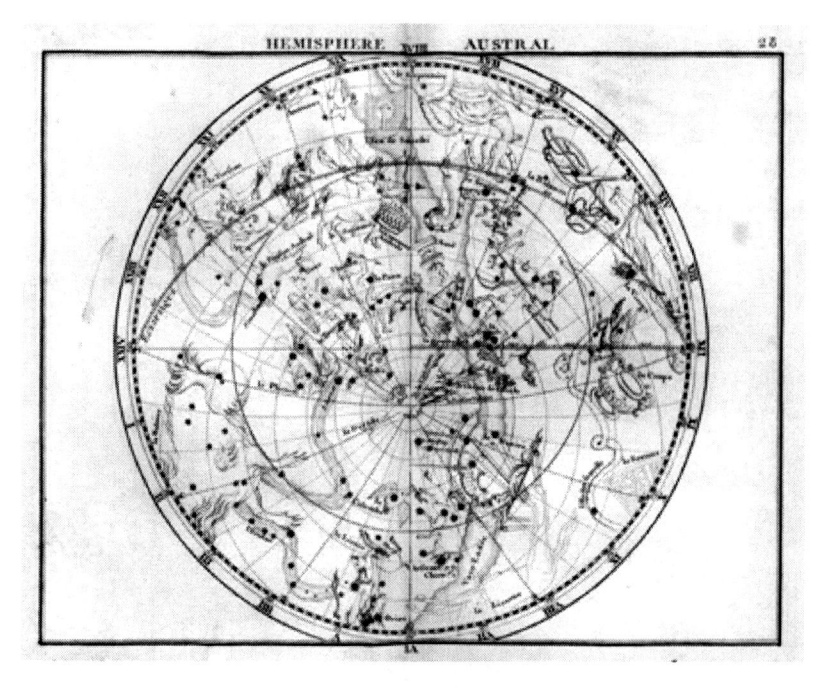

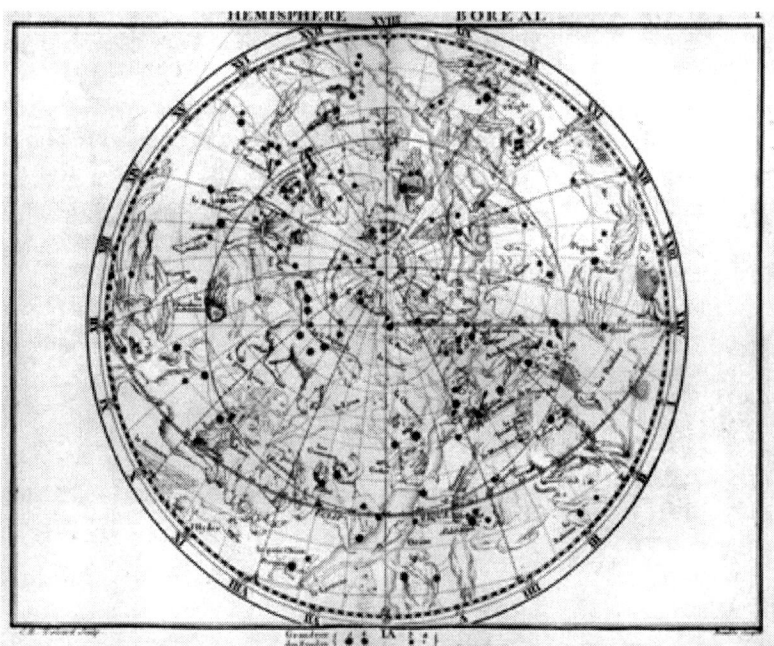

ATLAS CÉLESTE DE FLAMSTÉED

In the Temple of Hathor in Tentyra (Dendera) in Egypt; one of the oldest circular Zodiacs in the world (circa 50 BC) is carved on the ceiling of Osiris's chamber. The oldest circular Zodiac in Britain is the *'Birth of Mithras'* Zodiac, currently in Newcastle University Museum's antiquities collection.

This image is from John Cole's Treatise- *The Circular Zodiac of Tentyra, in Egypt.* As shown in *The Secret Teachings of All Ages* by Manly P Hall, (1928).

OPENING & CLOSING RITES

Kore Kosmon by Julian Dourado.

INTRODUCTION

"Then as soon as my tears would suffer me to speak, I began by saying, 'Most sacred and excellent father, since this is life, as Africanus tells me, why do I remain on the earth, and not rather hasten to come to you?' 'Not so,' said he; 'for unless the God who has for his temple all that you now behold, shall have freed you from this prison of the body, there can be no entrance for you hither. Men have indeed been brought into being on this condition, that they should guard the globe which you see in the midst of this temple, which is called the earth; and a soul has been given to them from those eternal fires which you call constellations and stars, which, globed and round, animated with god-derived minds, complete their courses and move

through their orbits with amazing speed. You, therefore, Publius, and all rightly disposed men are bound to retain the soul in the body's keeping, nor without the command of him who gave it to you to depart from the life appointed for man, lest you may seem to have taken flight from human duty as assigned by God'"

- Scipio's Dream by Cicero.[1]

All the rites in this book have the following opening and closing which is specifically designed for emphasis on the stellar nature of the intended ceremonies.

It is useful to set up your altar and working space properly, and each chapter provides some suggestions on what the ritual set up for each rite could be.

The opening has three steps:

Step 1 of the Opening

i) The first step in the opening is a visualisation to allow the formation of a connection to earth and heavens. This is called the *Celestial and Earth Tree Meditation,* which is a combination of several similar opening visualisations: Druid body of light exercise, the Kabbalistic cross (from the lesser banishing ritual of the pentagram), Nordic Seething (Seidr), and the Wiccan Tree meditation. The *Celestial and Earth Tree Meditation* here combines elements from all of these.

Step 2 of the Opening

ii) The second step in the opening is the calling on the four Persian Royal Stars or the Stellar Chieftains. As this forms an important part of each rite, the Persian Royal Stars and related material are discussed briefly here. The four Royal Stars were recognised around 3000 BC and were used as a marker of the seasons, the equinoxes and the solstices. However, due to the Procession of the Equinoxes, their prominence has shifted as seasonal markers.

The four Stellar Chieftains or Persian Royal Stars, are the Watchers and the Guardians of sky, these are thought to be:

East: Aldebaran, eye of the constellation Taurus. It was associated with the vernal equinox. Due to the procession of the Equinoxes it is now associated with Beltane, 1st May.

South: Regulus, in the constellation Leo. It was associated with the summer solstice. Due to the procession of the Equinoxes it is now associated with the festival of Lammas, 1st August.

West: Antares, in the constellation Scorpio, and heel of the Serpent Bearer (Ophiuchus). It was associated with the autumnal equinox. Due to the procession of the Equinoxes it is now associated with Samhain, 1st November.

North: Fomalhaut, in the stream of the Water Bearer (Aquarius) constellations, and in the head of the Southern Fish (Pisces Australis). It was associated with the winter solstice. Due to the procession of the Equinoxes it is now associated with Imbolc, 1st February.

One of the references to the Royal Stars is in the Persian *Pahlavi Texts* we read:

"0. On the formation of the luminaries.

1. Aûharmazd produced illumination between the sky and the earth, the constellation stars and those also not of the constellations, then the moon, and afterwards the sun, as I shall relate.

2. First he produced, the celestial sphere, and the constellation stars are assigned to it by him; especially these twelve whose names are Varak (the Lamb), Tôrâ (the Bull), Dô-patkar (the Two-figures or Gemini), Kalakang (the Crab), Sêr (the Lion), Khûsak (Virgo), Tarâzûk (the Balance), Gazdûm (the Scorpion), Nîmâsp (the Centaur or Sagittarius), Vahîk (Capricornus), Dûl (the Waterpot), and Mâhîk (the Fish);

3. which, from their original creation, were divided into the twenty-eight subdivisions of the astronomers, of which the names are Padêvar, Pêsh-Parvîz, Parviz, Paha, Avêsar, Besn, Rakhvad, Taraha, Avra, Nahn, Miyân, Avdem, Mâshâha, Spûr, Husru, Srob, Nur, Gêl, Garafsa, Varant, Gau, Goî, Muru, Bunda, Kahtsar, Vaht, Miyân, Kaht

4. And all his original creations, residing in the world, are committed to them; so that when the destroyer arrives they overcome the adversary and their own persecution, and the creatures are saved from those adversities.

5. As a specimen of a warlike army, which is destined for battle, they have ordained every single constellation of those 6480 thousand small stars as assistance; **and among those constellations four chieftains, appointed on the four sides, are leaders.**

> 6. On the recommendation of those chieftains the many unnumbered stars are specially assigned to the various quarters and various places, as the united strength and appointed power of those constellations.
>
> 7. As it is said that Tîstar is the chieftain of the east, Satavês the chieftain of the west, Vanand the chieftain of the south, and Haptôk-rîng the chieftain of the north.
>
> 8. The great one which they call a Gâh (period of the day), which they say is the great one of the middle of the sky, till just before the destroyer came was the midday (or south) one of the five, that is, the Rapîtvîn.
>
> 9. Aûharmazd performed the spiritual Yazisn ceremony with the archangels (ameshêspendân) in the Rapîtvîn Gâh, and in the Yazisn he supplied every means necessary for overcoming the adversary.
>
> 10. He deliberated with the consciousness (bôd) and guardian spirits (fravâhar) of men, and the omniscient wisdom, brought forward among men, spoke thus: Which seems to you the more advantageous, when I shall present you to the world? that you shall contend in a bodily form with the fiend (drûg), and the fiend shall perish, and in the end I shall have you prepared again perfect and immortal, and in the end give you back to the world, and you will be wholly immortal, un-decaying, and undisturbed; or that it be always necessary to provide you protection from the destroyer?
>
> 11. Thereupon, the guardian spirits of men became of the same opinion with the omniscient wisdom about going to the world, on account of the evil that comes upon them, in the world, from the fiend (drûg) Ahriman, and their becoming, at last, again unpersecuted by the adversary, perfect, and immortal, in the future existence, for ever and everlasting."[2]

There is a significant debate about the exact identification of the Persian Royal Stars, and some writers (George A. Davies) view the four Persian Royal Stars being as Tîstar: Sirius in the East, Vanand: Antares (Scorpio) West, Satavês: Fomalhaut (Aquarius) in the South, and Haptôk-rîng: Great Bear/Plough in the North.

However, here we follow more popular convention (by Jean Bailly) of the Persian Royal Stars as East: Aldebaran (Taurus), South: Regulus (Leo), West: Antares (Scorpio), and North: Fomalhaut (Aquarius).

The two red stars of Aldebaran and Antares face each other and the two white stars of Regulus and Fomalhaut face each other. This forms a celestial alchemy of a white light/line axis and a red light/line axis crossing + each other in mid heaven. When we take the Roman astrologer Marcus Manilius' god and goddess pairing of constellations into account we can see the Leo (Jupiter) is paired with Aquarius (Juno), they are king and queen of heaven: the South-North white axis (and Solstices circa 3000 BC). Taurus (Venus Goddess of love) is paired with Scorpio (Mars God of war), the most fiery and passionate pairing: East-West red axis (and Equinoxes circa 3000 BC).

The theme of naming and numbering of the stars is also seen in Christianity in the *Book of Enoch*:

> *'I beheld the celestial stars come forth. I numbered them as they proceeded out of the gate, and wrote them all down, as they came out one by one according to their number. I wrote down their names altogether, their times and their seasons, as the angel Uriel, who was with me, pointed them out to me. He showed them all to me and wrote down an account of them. He also wrote down for me their names, their regulations and their operations.' -Enoch 32:2-3.*

The four Persian Royal Stars also feature in Christianity. According to John P. Pratt in *The Lion and Unicorn Testify of Christ Part II: The Four Royal Stars*:

> "*Thus, Enoch was shown all the governing stars and learned their names. Now let us turn to identifying the four angels represented by the four principal or 'royal' stars. These stars are first, Regulus, the bright star at the heart of the Lion. The second star is Antares, the red star at the heart of the Scorpion, and also in the foot of the Serpent Bearer. The third star is Fomalhaut, the bright star both in the head of the Southern Fish and also in the stream of water being poured out by the Water Bearer. The fourth royal star is Aldebaran, the flaming red eye of the white Bull.*" [3]

The four faces of the Cherubim (the Biblical *Book of Ezekiel* 1:10, 10:14) are the four Royal Stars. Their symbols are the lion, eagle/serpent, man and wild ox (unicorn).[4] The four Royal Stars (four creatures), are said to found on each side of the throne of God (the Biblical *Book of Revelation* 4:7).

The description of Cherubim is of interest, as is where Ezekiel had his vision, in the land of the Chaldeans, further emphasising the importance of the *Chaldean Oracles*.

Ezekiel, chapter 1

> "*1: Now it came to pass in the thirtieth year, in the fourth month, in the fifth day of the month, as I was among the*

*captives by the river of Chebar, that the heavens were opened, and I saw visions of God.
2: In the fifth day of the month, which was the fifth year of king Jehoiachin's captivity,
3: The word of the Lord came expressly unto Ezekiel the priest, the son of Buzi, in the land of the Chaldeans by the river Chebar; and the hand of the Lord was there upon him.
4: And I looked, and, behold, a whirlwind came out of the north, a great cloud, and a fire infolding itself, and a brightness was about it, and out of the midst thereof as the colour of amber, out of the midst of the fire.
5: Also out of the midst thereof came the likeness of four living creatures. And this was their appearance; they had the likeness of a man.
6: And every one had four faces, and every one had four wings.
7: And their feet were straight feet; and the sole of their feet was like the sole of a calf's foot: and they sparkled like the colour of burnished brass.
8: And they had the hands of a man under their wings on their four sides; and they four had their faces and their wings.
9: Their wings were joined one to another; they turned not when they went; they went every one straight forward.
10: As for the likeness of their faces, they four had the face of a man, and the face of a lion, on the right side: and they four had the face of an ox on the left side; they four also had the face of an eagle.
11: Thus were their faces: and their wings were stretched upward; two wings of every one were joined one to another, and two covered their bodies.
12: And they went every one straight forward: whither the spirit was to go, they went; and they turned not when they went.
13: As for the likeness of the living creatures, their appearance was like burning coals of fire, and like the appearance of lamps: it went up and down among the living creatures; and the fire was bright, and out of the fire went forth lightning.
14: And the living creatures ran and returned as the appearance of a flash of lightning.
15: Now as I beheld the living creatures, behold one wheel upon the earth by the living creatures, with his four faces...."[5] Bible, King James. Ezekiel.*

The four Royal Stars and their constellations also feature in Christianity as the four Evangelists as well as the Cherubim. The symbols for the four Evangelists are: Matthew as Human/Angel (Aquarius), Mark as Lion (Leo), Luke as Ox (Taurus), John as Eagle (Aquila/Scorpio). Those familiar with the Golden Dawn system and Rider-Waite tarot deck, will recognise the four Cherubim on the four corners of the World card and Wheel of Fortune card in the pack.

The snake or cloth is the constellation Draco which wraps around the Pole Star (Little Bear), the *Axis Mundi*.

From being worshipped on the tops of Babylonian Ziggurats, the four Royal Stars found their way into ancient Greco-Roman astrology and eventually into Christianity and Kabbalah. Down the centuries they become incorporated as Watchtowers by John Dee in his Enochian magic, and finally reaching modern day magicians in the form of the four lords of Watchtowers in Wicca and the Golden Dawn or Watchers (Grigori) in Stregheria.

As part of the opening and closing of each rite the recitation of the Zoroastrian prayer *'Namaz-i chahar nemag'* (praise to the four directions) is used.[6] The ideal and concept of *Asha* (*'Truth'*) mentioned in this prayer is similar to the Sufi concept of the divine name *Al-Haqq* (in Arabic: *'the Truth'*). This is the divine truth reflecting an understanding of the nature of reality.

Step 3 of the Opening

iii) The third step in the opening is the reading of the *Orphic Hymn to the Stars*. Hence the three steps of the opening come together. The *Orphic Hymns* are a set of pre-classical poetic compositions, attributed to Orpheus the founder of Greek Mysteries. He was thought to be a poet and musician of antiquity, and the inventor of the lyre. He is said to have brought the arts and alphabet to mankind, his music was charming and enchanting to an extent that all animals and even stones and rocks would be moved on hearing it. The *Orphic Hymns* were probably composed by several different poets rather than just one person, perhaps Orpheus was a title given to great poets and not just one person.

STANDARD OPENING

Note: *This hence forth will be referred to as the 'standard opening', and used as the opening for every rite in this book.*

The directions of the four Royal Stars or guardians should be determined for the day/time/ location/latitude you are performing the rite using a Planisphere or Star Globe. If you are unable to determine the actual directions of the four stars, then the default setting to use is: East: Aldebaran, South: Regulus, West: Antares, North: Fomalhaut. The four star directions are points in a sphere and not just in a circle of horizon around you, that is the four stars could be above and below you as well as to the front and back of you.

- ⊕ All begin with the Celestial and Earth Tree meditation mediation to root yourself to earth before reaching for the stars.

Celestial and Earth Tree meditation

Standing upright with your hands at your sides, visualise yourself growing roots into the earth and making a connection. Allow roots to come out of your feet into the earth and then feel the earth energy rise up, to your ankles, calves, knees, thighs, and groin, up the spine, higher up the spine to the back of the neck. Feel the energy filling the front of your body, stomach, chest and then down the arms. Next, feel the energy reaching your head and filling it. Imagine yourself as tree, with roots in soil and in the past. Your tree trunk is solid in the present. Your branches are reaching the future and high into the night sky and basking in starlight. Raise your arms upwards towards the stars, like branches reaching for the light, and allow the starlight to enter you. Visualise the shining starlight entering the top of your head, filling your head, neck and upper body with starlight. Next feel the earth energy from below and stellar energy from above mixing and mingling inside you. Visualise yourself as a bright shining star that stands with its feet on the earth and head in the heavens.

Feel yourself centred and connected to both sky and earth. Then visualise the sphere.

- ⊕ All hold hands and cast circle as expansion of the meditation forming a sacred constellation.
- ⊕ Each person is visualising being a Star, when you hold hands, the stars begin connecting and a constellation is formed.
- ⊕ Next call on the four Stellar Chieftains or Persian Royal Stars. These are the Watchers and Guardians of sky. First recite the *'praise to the four directions'* and visualize the appropriate constellation for each direction and call on the Royal Stars using your own words.
- ⊕ Recite the *'Namaz-i chahar nemag'* (praise to the four directions) once facing East, once West, once South, and once North, respectively:

"*Homage to these places and these lands, and for these pastures, and these abodes with their hay-racks, and for the waters, land, and plants, and for this earth and for your heaven, and for the Asha-owning wind, and for the stars, moon, and sun, and for the eternal stars without beginning, and self-disposing, and for all the Asha-owning creatures of Spenta Mainyu (the bounteous spirit), male and female, the regulators of Asha."*

- ⊕ When facing East after reciting the *'praise to the four directions'* call on the star Aldebaran, the red eye of the constellation Taurus (earth elemental sign), who was associated with the vernal equinox. Visualize a great Bull as part of the celestial sphere.
- ⊕ When facing West after reciting the *'praise to the four directions'* call on the star Antares, in the constellation Scorpio (water elemental sign), and heel of the Serpent Bearer (Ophiuchus), who was associated with the autumnal equinox. Visualize a Man holding a serpent standing above a scorpion as part of the celestial sphere.
- ⊕ When facing South after reciting the *'praise to the four directions'* call on Regulus, in the constellation Leo (fire elemental sign), who was associated with the summer solstice. Visualize a Lion as part of the celestial sphere.

(IMAGE FROM ATLAS CÉLESTE DE FLAMSTÉED)

37 | S t e l l a r   M a g i c

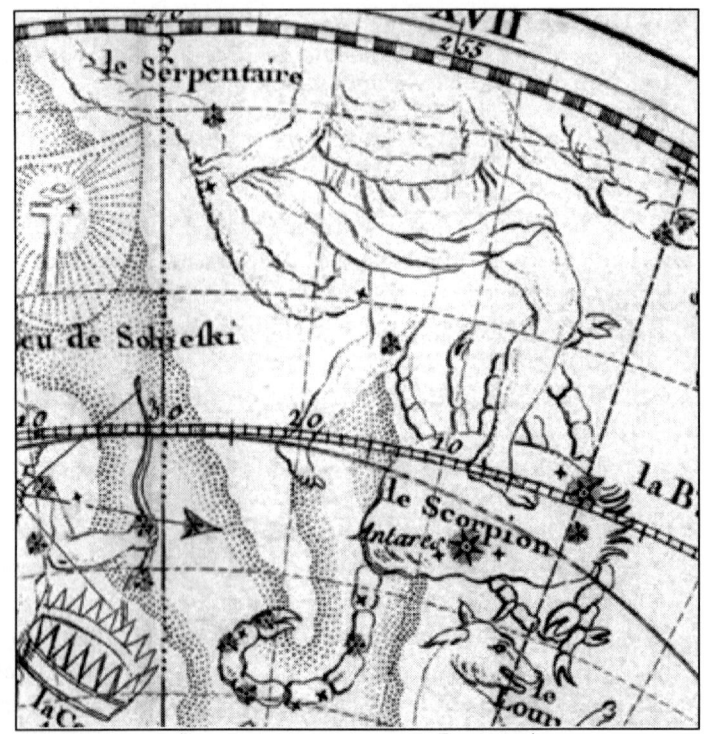

(IMAGE FROM ATLAS CÉLESTE DE FLAMSTÉED)

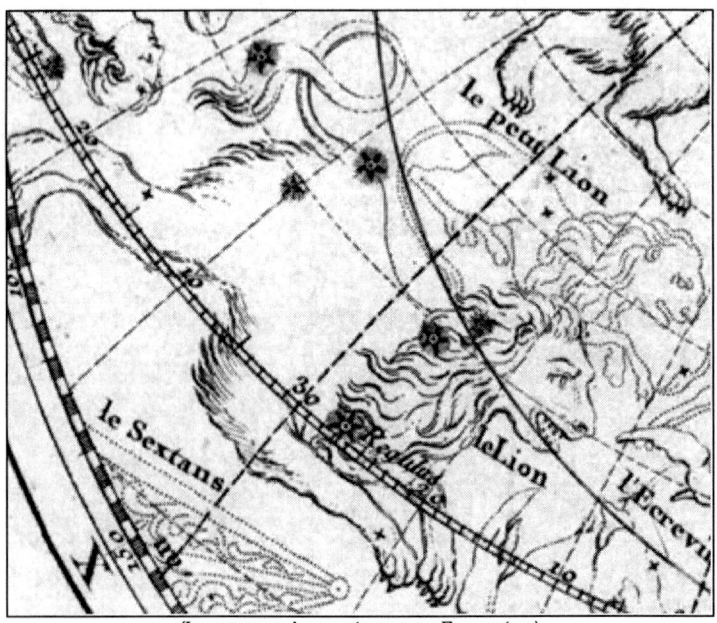

(IMAGE FROM ATLAS CÉLESTE DE FLAMSTÉED)

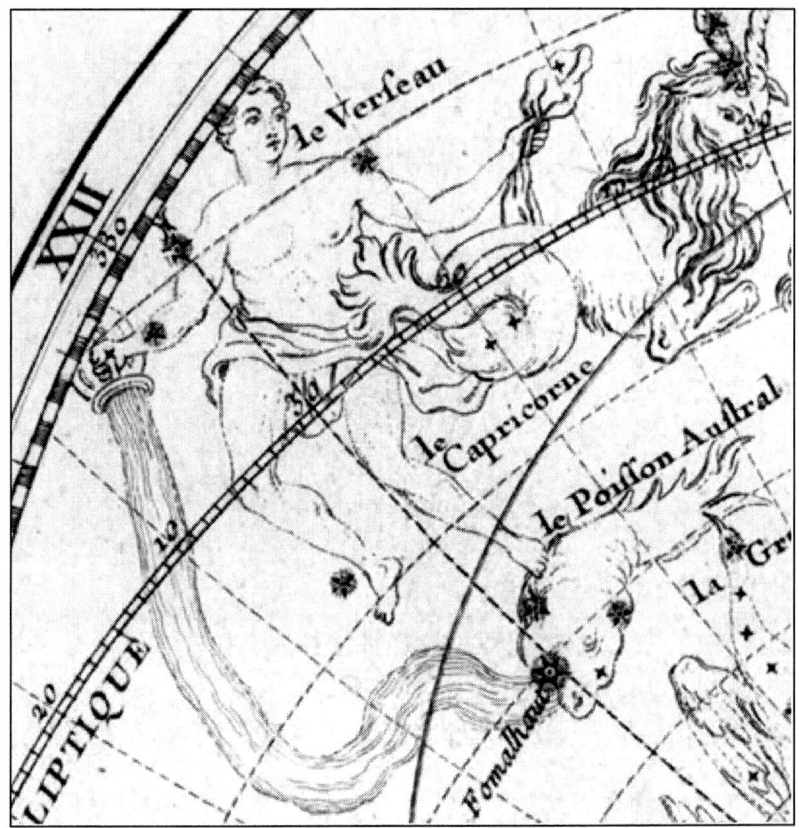

(IMAGE FROM ATLAS CÉLESTE DE FLAMSTÉED)

⊕ When facing North after reciting the *'praise to the four directions'* call on the star Fomalhaut, which is in the stream of the Water Bearer (Aquarius) constellation (air elemental sign), and in the head of the Southern Fish (Pisces Australis). Fomalhaut was associated with the winter solstice. Visualize a Man pouring water from a cup as part of the celestial sphere.

⊕ Maintain visualisation of the four Royal Stars, as part of a sphere.

⊕ After having invoked the four Royal Stars, the following Orphic hymn is recited:

To The Stars
(The Hymns of Orpheus)

> With holy voice we call the stars on high,
> Pure sacred lights and genii of the sky.
> Celestial stars, the progeny of Night,
> In whirling circles beaming far your light,
> Refulgent rays around the heavens ye throw,
> Eternal fires, the source of all below.
> With flames significant of Fate ye shine,
> And aptly rule for men a path divine.
> In seven bright zones ye run with wandering flames,
> And heaven and earth compose your lucid frames:
> With course unwearied, pure and fiery bright
> Forever shining thro' the veil of Night.
> Hail twinkling, joyful, ever wakeful fires!
> Propitious shine on all my just desires;
> These sacred rites regard with conscious rays,
> And begin our works devoted to your praise [7]

STANDARD CLOSING

Note: This hence forth will be referred to as the *'standard closing'*, and used as the closing for every rite in this book.

- ⊕ Saying of thanks to spirits of the place. This is thanking the genius loci, the protective spirit of a place.
- ⊕ Sending of Blessings. This is an act of sending of some of the energy of the rite to help those who need it. For example, this can be sending healing.
- ⊕ Final thanks to main constellation that was worked with and was intent of the rite.
- ⊕ Say Thanks to the Stars, Repeat *"To the Stars"* (The Hymns of Orpheus)
- ⊕ Finish the rite by reciting the *'Namaz-i chahar nemag'* again, in reverse order this time, thanking each Royal Star in turn in your own words. First facing North, then South, West, and East, respectively:

"*Homage to these places and these lands, and for these pastures, and these abodes with their hay-racks, and for the waters, land, and plants, and for this earth and for your heaven, and for the Asha-owning wind, and for the stars, moon, and sun, and for the eternal stars without beginning, and self-*

> *disposing, and for all the Asha-owning creatures of Spenta Mainyu, male and female, the regulators of Asha".'*

It is recommended to have something to eat and drink after a rite. Finally clear the space where you performed your rite, and if outdoors, make you sure you are following the country code: *leave only footprints, take only pictures.*

References
1. *Scipio's Dream* by Cicero, Translated, with an Introduction and Notes by Andrew P. Peabody.
2. *Pahlavi Texts, Part I Sacred Books of the East, Vol. 5* translated by E.W. West 1880.
3. *The Lion and Unicorn Testify of Christ Part II: The Four Royal Stars* by John P. Pratt, in *Meridian Magazine*, Dec. 5, 2001.
4. The *Lion and Unicorn Testify of Christ Part I: The Cornerstone Constellations* by John P. Pratt, in *Meridian Magazine*, Nov. 8, 2001.
5. Bible, King James. *Ezekiel*, from the Holy Bible, King James version Electronic Text Center, University of Virginia Library.
6. *Namaz-i Chahar Nemag, Avesta: Khorda Avesta* (Book of Common Prayer) Translation by James Darmesteter, from *Sacred Books of the East*, American Edition, 1898.
7. *The Hymns of Orpheus* translated by Thomas Taylor, 1792.

For discussion on alternative naming and identification of the four Persian Royal Stars see: *The so-called Royal Stars of Persia* by Davis, G. A., Jr., in *Popular Astronomy*, Vol. 53, p.149-159 April 1945.

Notes:

THE CONSTELLATION ORION:

HORUS

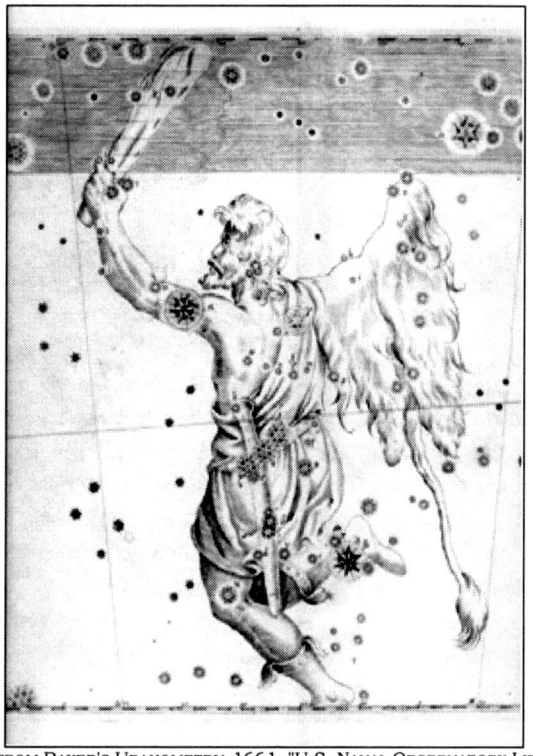

ORION FROM BAYER'S URANOMETRIA 1661, "U.S. NAVAL OBSERVATORY LIBRARY".

INTRODUCTION

*"The Persian, zealous to reject
Altar and image of inclusive walls
And roofs of temples built by human hands-
The loftiest heights, ascending from their tops
With myrtle-wreathed tiara on his brow
Presented sacrifice to moon and stars,
And to winds and mother elements
And the whole circle of heaven for him
A sensitive existence of a God."*
— William Wordsworth (Excursion Book-IV)

Orion was a mighty hunter who has many myths attributed to him; Orion was also the son of the Sea God Neptune. He was a giant who was able to walk in the sea, with his head above the water. In the night sky the Greeks saw him holding a club in one hand and holding a lion skin or shield in the other, he was fighting the bull constellation Taurus. He is also chasing the constellation the Pleiades, the seven sisters whom he was enamoured with, and he hunts the Hare constellation. The constellation Scorpio is positioned so that it opposes him. Sagittarius was placed next to the Scorpion; with his bow aimed at the scorpion's heart, should he try to move towards Orion. The Orion-Scorpio story echoes the astronomical phenomenon that Orion and the constellation Scorpio each rise as the other sets. Orion is the brightest constellation, so bright that it was said: night, mistaking him for day, folds her dark wings. Orion is the winter constellation *par excellence*. The constellation Orion is one of the oldest constellations described by man, the Orion constellation is invoked in the Babylonian *A Prayer to Gods of the Night* (circa 1700 BC).

Orion evolved in the view of the Romans to be armed with a sword, and a baldric, wore the military belt and was seen as a prime example of a warrior. He portended war by making his sword flare brightly in the sky. Those born when Orion was visible or rising were said to have the characteristics of officers and soldiers. The influence of Orion on the Roman army is discussed in *Mithras-Orion: Greek Hero and Roman Army God* by Michael P. Speidel.

There are a number of variations on the Greek/Roman legend of Orion. According to Aratus' *Phaenomena,* Orion makes some advances toward Artemis which anger her and in her rage she raises all the animals including the scorpion against him. In the ensuing battle the scorpion fatally wounds Orion, and even now as the Scorpio rises in the East, Orion flees in the Western horizon.

In another version of the story:

> "*Orion loved Merope, the daughter of Oenopion, king of Chios, and sought her in marriage. He cleared the island of wild beasts, and brought the spoils of the chase as presents to his beloved; but as Oenopion constantly deferred his consent, Orion attempted to gain possession of the maiden by violence. Her father, incensed at this conduct, having made Orion drunk, deprived him of his sight and cast him out on the seashore. The blinded hero followed the sound, of a Cyclops' hammer till he reached Lemnos, and came to the forge of Vulcan, who, taking pity on him, gave him Kedalion, one of his men, to be his guide to the abode of the sun. Placing Kedalion on his shoulders,*

Orion proceeded to the east, and there meeting the sun-god, was restored to sight by his beam.
After this he dwelt as a hunter with Diana, with whom he was a favourite, and it is even said she was about to marry him. Her brother was highly displeased and often chided her, but to no purpose. One day, observing Orion wading through the sea with his head just above the water, Apollo pointed it out to his sister and maintained that she could not hit that black thing on the sea. The archer-goddess discharged a shaft with fatal aim. The waves rolled the dead body of Orion to the land, and bewailing her fatal error with many tears, Diana placed him among the stars, where he appears as a giant, with a girdle, sword, lion's skin, and club. Sirius, his dog, follows him, and the Pleiades fly before him.
The Pleiades were the daughters of Atlas, and nymphs of Diana's train. One day Orion saw them and became enamoured and pursued them. In their distress they prayed to the gods to change their form, and Jupiter in pity turned them into pigeons, and then made them a constellation in the sky. Though their number was seven, only six stars are visible, for Electra, one of them, it is said left her place that she might not behold the ruin of Troy, for that city was founded by her son Dardanus. The sight had such an effect on her sisters that they have looked pale ever since."[1]

In another version of the story, when Orion threatened to kill all the beasts on the earth, Gaia (Earth) became angry and created a giant scorpion that killed Orion with its sting. Zeus on the request of Artemis and Leto placed Orion in the sky and to mark his bravery placed Scorpio in the sky also.

The origin of the name Orion relates to one of his birth stories, in which Hyrieus of Thebes asks for the gift of fatherhood of his guests Mercury and Jupiter. He offered them an Ox for their feast and Mercury and Jupiter accepted the offering and instructed him to remove the ox hide, they then urinate on the ox hide and instructed him to bury it. Sometime later a boy was born who Hyrieus called Urion (*'urine born'*)[2]. The rising and setting of the constellation of Orion was thought to be followed by storms and rain.

There has been a great deal written about Orion by modern writers. For example the book *The Orion Mystery* by Robert Bauval and Adrian Gilbert, which looks at the link between the positions of the Giza pyramids and the major stars of Orion. The Giza site offers a good example of archaeoastronomy. Built around 3000 BC, the pyramids are aligned to the compass directions, each side faces east, west, north, and south perfectly. Furthermore, at 3000 BC the pole star was Thuban in the constellation Draco, meaning passages in the north face of the pyramids emerge to point at this star. One theory is that the Giza site was designed to mirror the sky, the three pyramids represent the belt stars of the constellation Orion, the Sphinx is the constellation Leo and the Nile the Milky Way. Orion here is seen as Osiris, the God of the underworld and resurrection.[3]

However, the view of Orion in the Egyptian religion being Osiris is a controversial one, as some hold the view that Orion was seen as Horus, the son of Osiris. This controversy has little effect on the archaeoastronomy of the Giza site, as either way it demonstrates the importance of the stars to Egyptian religion.

What we are concerned with here with is working with the constellation Orion and using Egyptian sources as example. The question of Orion being Osiris or Horus needs further examination. While father and son both have close links, there are also significant differences. For an answer to this, we will use Plutarch as our source:

> 'For when the Egyptians themselves tell us that Hermes had one hand shorter than another, that Typhon was of red complexion, Horus fair, and Osiris black, does not this show that they were of the human species, and subject to the same accidents as all other men? Nay, they go farther, and even declare the particular work in which each was engaged whilst alive. Thus they say that Osiris was a general, that Canopus, from whom the star took its name, was a pilot, and that the ship which the Greeks call Argo, being made in imitation of the ship of Osiris, was, in honour of him, turned into a constellation and placed near Orion and the Dog-star, the former being sacred to Horus and the latter to Isis.'[4]

The above passage assigns Horus to Orion, Isis to Sirius, and Osiris to Canopus/Argo. Further arguments for Orion being Horus and Canopus being Osiris can be found in *The Canopus Revelation: The Stargate of the Gods and the Ark of Osiris* by Philip Coppens.

In my view, the Greek/Roman myths of Orion better align with myths of Horus than with those of Osiris. For example both the Greek/Roman Orion and the Egyptian Horus are great warriors. Orion is chasing the daughters of Atlas, the seven sisters: the constellation Pleiades, while Horus is partnered with Hathor (The Seven Hathors being the Pleiades). Orion loses his sight and Horus loses an eye, both have their vision healed. Finally, Orion and Horus both get bitten by a scorpion.

Some other world myths also see Orion as a warrior. For example, in the *Epic of Gilgamesh*, the Bull of Heaven (the constellation Taurus) is killed by Gilgamesh (Orion) and his friend

Enkidu. In short, the constellation Orion, be it the Greek Giant hunter, the Roman soldier, or the Egyptian Horus warrior, all play on the same warrior god theme. The following modern rite is designed to connect with the constellation Orion using Greek, Roman and Egyptian texts, with a focus on Horus. One part of the rite includes a visualisation of Temple of Horus at Edfu, and it is recommended that the participants memorise the structure and map of the temple beforehand.

P. Nabarz at Temple of Horus at Edfu, (note Mithras Tauroctony on the t-shirt)
photo by Tony M.

P. Nabarz at Temple of Horus at Edfu, in the inner chamber the sanctuary of Horus, Photo by Tony M.

The Temple at Edfu contains images honouring Hathor and Horus together as partners and was part of the *'The Festival of the Beautiful Reunion'*. The Seven Hathors are an aspect of Hathor, they were seven women in ritual dress who were present at childbirth and would one by one tell the child's fortune. They were identified as the Pleiades. Hathor means the *'house of Horus'*. Some view Min as the constellation Orion, however Min became linked with Horus, who was also a God of the raised arm (shape of Orion).

This is the first rite in this book as we are currently in the Aeon of Horus according to the Thelemic view, hence is it appropriate to begin with a rite to Horus-Orion.

It is also worth noting that the Orion Nebula constellation (M42) is 1500 light years away from us, which means the light we are seeing and drawing upon left Orion at 500 AD, a time in earth when the Roman Empire was beginning to collapse and the city of Constantinople was just beginning to rise. In stellar magic there is an element of journeying in time as well as space!

As part of your preparation, a visit to the virtual online Temple of Edfu is recommended to help familiarise yourself with the Temple. This is available via the Edfu project site.[5]

ORION-HORUS RITE

Set up
- Location: a place with good visibility of the stars. (If indoors with Stellar maps on altar).
- Candles or tea lights to be lit and placed on altar in shape of constellation Orion
- Central fire lit (if needed due to cold) but kept to a size not to affect the night vision too much.
- Time to perform this rite is determined using a Star-globe or Star-chart to ensure visibility of the Orion constellation.
- Clothing: sensible outdoor clothing & footwear.
- A Sistrum.
- Altar cloth to have stars on it if possible.
- A Hawk feather if possible.
- Offerings to Horus.
- Face paint or body paint e.g. Henna or Woad or commercial ones from party shops. Henna or Woad paint stay on for a while, so more washable body paint might better if you don't want to be marked for a while.
- Food and drink to share.

Use the body paint (e.g. Henna) to draw the stars of Orion (as large dots) on your body, in positions shown in usual pictures of Orion. The two upper stars are on the shoulders (Betelgeuse left shoulder). The three stars of Orion's belt are on the waist, the two lower stars of the sword's scabbard are on the right thigh, and the two bottom stars are on the knees (Rigel left knee, Saiph right knee).

Opening
- The standard opening mentioned in the chapter *'opening and closing of rites'* is used here followed by:
- Light the candles which are set in shape of the stars of the constellation of Orion.
- Declare your intent as wanting to connect with Orion and to *'draw down'* the power of Orion into yourself (if that is part of your intent).

AN ORION-HORUS ALTAR (PHOTO BY P. NABARZ)

⊕ While looking at the constellation, next take the stance of Orion, right arm raised like holding a sword, left arm holding a shield as figure:

Orion
HYGINUS - POETICON ASTRONOMICON

Meditate on the constellation of Orion, while standing in this position for a few minutes.

When you feel ready, recite the following hymn to Horus. Before you recite, visualise a door in front of you which has the stars of Orion painted on it.

> "101. A hymn of praise to Horus to glorify him, which is to be said over the waters and over the land.
> Thoth spoke and this god recited the following:
> 'Homage to you, god, son of a god. Homage to you, heir, son of an heir. Homage to you, bull, son of a bull, who was brought forth by a holy goddess. Homage to you, Horus, who comes forth from Osiris, and was brought forth by the goddess Isis. I recite your words of power, I speak with your magical utterance. I pronounce a spell in your own words, which your heart has created, and all the spells and incantations which have come forth from your mouth, which your father Geb commanded you [to recite], and your mother Nuit gave to you, and the majesty of the Governor of Sekhem taught you to make use of for your protection, in order to double (or, repeat) your protective formulae, to shut the mouth of every reptile which is in heaven, and on the earth, and in the waters, to make men and women to live, to make the gods to be at peace [with you], and to make Ra to employ his magical spells through your chants of praise. Come to me this day, quickly, quickly, as you work the paddle of the Boat of the god. Drive you away from me every lion on the plain, and every crocodile in the waters, and all mouths which bite (or, sting) in their holes. Make you them before me like the stone of the mountain, like a broken pot lying about in a quarter of the town. Dig you out from me the poison which was raised and is in every member of him that is under the knife. Keep you watch over him by means of your words. Verily let your name be invoked this day. Let your power (qefau) come into being in him. Exalt you your magical powers. Make me to live and him whose throat is closed up. Then shall mankind give you praise, and the righteous shall give thanks unto your forms. And all the gods likewise shall invoke you, and in truth your name shall be invoked this day. I am Horus of Shetenu.
> O you who art in the cavern, O you who art in the cavern. O you who art at the mouth of the cavern. O you who art on the way, O you who art on the way. O you who art at the mouth of the way. He is Urmer (Mnevis) who approaches every man and every beast. He is like the god Sep who is in Anu (Heliopolis). He is the Scorpion-[god] who is in the Great House (Het-ur). Bite him not, for he is Ra. Sting him not, for he is Thoth. Shoot you not your poison over him, for he is Nefertem. O every male serpent, O every female serpent, O every antesh (scorpion?) which bite with your mouths, and sting with your tails, bite him not with your mouths, and sting him not with your tails. Get ye

afar off from him, make ye not your fire to be against him, for he is the son of Osiris. Vomit ye.

I am Thoth, I have come from heaven to make protection of Horus, and to drive away the poison of the scorpion which is in every member of Horus. Your head is to you, Horus; it shall be stable under the Urert Crown. Your eye is to you, Horus, [for] you art Horus, the son of Geb, the Lord of the Two Eyes, in the midst of the Company of the gods. Your nose is to you, Horus, [for] you art Horus the Elder, the son of Ra, and you shall not inhale the fiery wind. Your arm is to you, Horus, great is your strength to slaughter the enemies of your father. Your two thighs are to you, Horus. Receive you the rank and dignity of your father Osiris. Ptah has balanced for you your mouth on the day of your birth. Your heart (or, breast) is to you, Horus, and the Disk makes your protection. Your eye is to you, Horus; your right eye is like Shu, and your left eye like Tefnut, who are the children of Ra. Your belly is to you, Horus, and the Children are the gods who are therein, and they shall not receive the essence (or, fluid) of the scorpion. Your strength is to you, Horus, and the strength of Seth shall not exist against you. Your phallus is to you, Horus, and you art Kamutef, the protector of his father, who makes an answer for his children in the course of every day. Your thighs are to you, Horus, and your strength shall slaughter the enemies of your father. Your calves are to you, Horus; the god Khnemu has built them, and the goddess Isis has covered them with flesh. The soles of your feet are to you, Horus, and the nations who fight with the bow (Peti) fall under your feet. You rule the South, North, West, and East, and you see like Ra. Say four times. And likewise him that is under the knife.

Beautiful god, Senetchem-ab-Ra-setep-[en]-Amen, son of Ra, Nekht-Heru-Hebit, thou art protected, and the gods and goddesses are protected, and conversely. Beautiful god, Senetchem-ab-Ra-setep-[en]-Ra, son of Ra, Nekht-Heru-Hebit, thou art protected, and Heru-Shet[enu], the great god, is protected, and conversely."[6]

Once you have recited the hymn visualise the door opening, step inside begin your journey to meet Horus-Orion.

Temple of Horus at Edfu

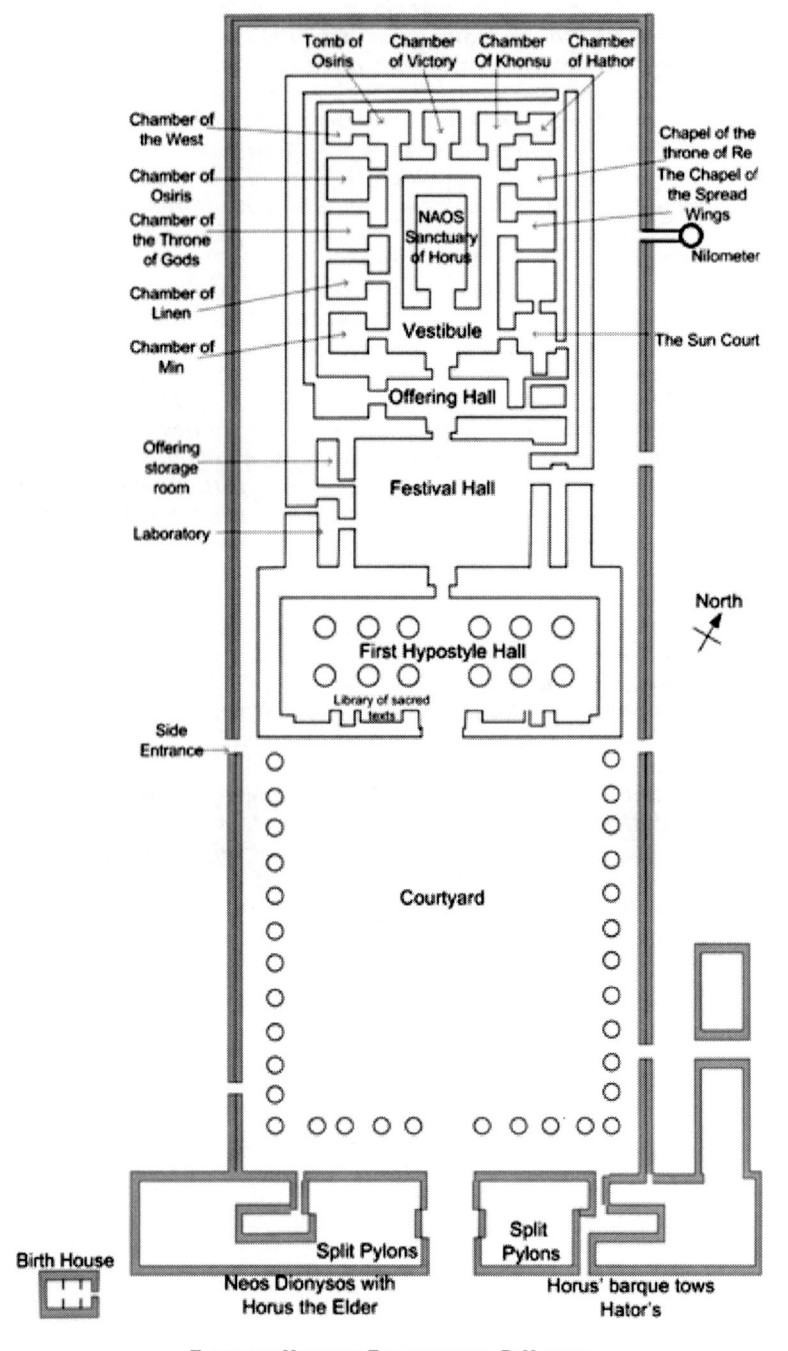

- Tomb of Osiris
- Chamber of Victory
- Chamber Of Khonsu
- Chamber of Hathor
- Chamber of the West
- Chamber of Osiris
- Chamber of the Throne of Gods
- Chamber of Linen
- Chamber of Min
- NAOS Sanctuary of Horus
- Vestibule
- Offering Hall
- Chapel of the throne of Re
- The Chapel of the Spread Wings
- Nilometer
- The Sun Court
- Offering storage room
- Festival Hall
- Laboratory
- First Hypostyle Hall
- Library of sacred texts
- Side Entrance
- North
- Courtyard
- Birth House
- Split Pylons
- Split Pylons
- Neos Dionysos with Horus the Elder
- Horus' barque tows Hator's

Temple of Horus at Edfu drawn by P. Nabarz

54 | Payam Nabarz

If you are planning to use an astral temple based on the Horus temple of Edfu, at this point, remember the map of the temple you have studied. Then visualise yourself once you step through the door to be standing outside the great temple in front of the split pylon. Make your way through the gate; you may meet a guardian at these gates who asks why you are entering. State your reason. In the courtyard take your time to look at the surroundings and the columns, make a mental note of what you see or hear, and when you are ready, make your way to the Hypostyle hall. There might be other pilgrims also making their way. As you enter the hypostyle hall you might be asked some questions by guardians of this doorway. Take your time and observe your surroundings, note any carvings and inscriptions on the wall. If you feel you want to continue make your way to the second hypostyle hall. Once more you may be asked questions by the guardians of the gateway. Again take time and pay attention to your surroundings. Once ready, enter the offering hall, here you will leave your offering and you might be asked what the offering symbolises to you. Then proceed to the heart of the temple out of the offering hall and toward the inner sanctum. There are a number of chambers here, follow your instinct and make your personal contact. Take your time.

Once ready, make your back from the inner sanctum to the offering hall, back through the hypostyle halls and to the court yard, and out through the split pylon to outside in front of the temple. Step through the door which had the Orion stars painted on and back to your circle.

> ⊕ Communion of Bread and Wine. Saying the following (from Grace before a Meal - Temple of Edfu (girdle-wall):
>
> "O Table-god (Atum), You have spat forth Shu from your mouth (...) O Table-god, may he (the king as Shu) give to You all that he will have dedicated, since he has become a god who is an emanation, alert, worshipful and powerful. (...) May he dedicate to You every good thing which You will give him, since he has become Heka. May he dedicate to You every good thing, food-offerings in abundance. May he set them before You and may You be content with them, may your Ka be content with them (...)
>
> Be satisfied and worshipful, O Living Falcon, Lord of the Two Lands, Lord of the Nobles, Lord of the common folk, Lord of the Seat of Ra, Lord of gods, through the offerings which this son of yours brings to You, this Worshipfulness of yours, this Ka of yours, this Heka of yours, this Ptah of yours, this Shu of yours, this Thoth of yours, this abundance of yours upon Earth. May You be content and worshipful with them. May your Ka be

content with them, and Your heart be content with them for ever."[7]

The standard closing mentioned in the chapter 'opening and closing of rites' is used here, followed by having something to eat and drink. Then clear the space.

References
1. *Bulfinch's mythology the age of fable or stories of gods and heroes* by Thomas Bulfinch, 1855.
2. *Star Myths of the Greeks and Romans: A Sourcebook* by Theony Condos. Phanes Press, U.S. Nov 1997.
3. *Astronomy: A Visual Guide* by Mark Garlick, Reader's Digest, 2005.
4. *Legends of the Gods The Egyptian Texts, edited with Translations* by E. A. Wallis Budge, London: Kegan Paul, Trench and Trübner & Co. Ltd 1912.
5. Edfu project site for 3D view of temple: http://www1.uni-hamburg.de/Edfu-Projekt/Edfu-Projekt%20-%20Multimedia%20engl.html
6. Based on: *Legends of the Gods the Egyptian Texts, edited with Translations* by E. A. Wallis Budge. London: Kegan Paul, Trench and Trübner & Co. Ltd, 1912, Lines 101 to 166.
7. *Grace before a Meal -Temple of Edfu* (girdle-wall) as quoted in 'Escaping Osiris ... O Osiris the king, who goes forth by night! by Wim van den Dungen' http://www.sofiatopia.org/maat/osiris.htm and also see Robert K. Ritner *'Practical Egyptian Magical Spells'*
http://oi.uchicago.edu/research/is/dinner.html

Further online resources:
For the Edfu project and a model of the Temple:
http://www1.uni-hamburg.de/Edfu-Projekt/Edfu-Projekt%20-%20Model.html

For details of Temple of Horus see:
http://www.touregypt.net/edfut.htm

Photographs of the Edfu temple available on:
http://www.galenfrysinger.com/egypt_edfu_temple_of_horus.htm
and
http://www.bluffton.edu/~sullivanm/egypt/edfu/edfu.html

Temple of Horus at Edfu drawn by P. Nabarz based on his site visit and http://www.touregypt.net/Map29.htm and http://lexicorient.com/egypt/edfu_m.htm

Further Reading:
The Canopus Revelation: The Stargate of the Gods and the Ark of Osiris, Philip Coppens, Adventures Unlimited Press, 2004.
Signs in the Sky: Astrological and Archaeological Evidence That We Are Entering a New Age, Adrian Gilbert, ARE Press, 2005.
Keeper of Genesis: A Quest for the Hidden Legacy of Mankind, Robert Bauval, William Heinemann Ltd, 2006.
The Orion Mystery: Unlocking the Secrets of the Pyramids, Robert Bauval, and Adrian Gilbert, Mandarin, 1995.
Mithras-Orion: Greek Hero and Roman Army God, Michael P Speidel, Brill, 1980.

Notes:

STAR SIRIUS:

SOTHIS & TISHTRYA (TIR)

Bust of Isis-Sothis-Demeter in Vatican City from Tivoli, Hadrian's Villa Palestra (131-138 AD). Photograph by Marie-Lan Nguyen/Wikimedia Commons.

INTRODUCTION

"I am a Star, whose Course is as your Course, shining anew from out of the depth. O thou Star-tamer!" - Mithras Liturgy.

"We sacrifice unto the rains of Tishtrya. We sacrifice unto the first star; we sacrifice unto the rains of the first star, whose eyesight is sound." - Tishtar Yasht (Zoroastrian Hymn to the Star Sirius).

The star Sirius or the Dog Star is part of the constellation Canis Major (Great Dog), in Greek myths he was seen as Orion's hunting dog. After the death of Orion, Diana placed Orion's dog in the sky at his heel to help with the stellar hunt. The star Sirius is part of the winter triangle; the two other points of the triangle are the star Betelgeuse in Orion and the star Procyon in Canis Minor. Sirius, the brightest star in the night sky can be located in the night sky by following an imaginary line from the three stars of Orion's belt to the left and down. The star Sirius is one of the oldest constellations described by man; the Fire Star is one of the stars in the Babylonian *A Prayer to Gods of the Night* (circa 1700 BC).

In Aratus' *Phaenomena,* Canis Major is described on its hind legs and on the tip of his jaw is the flaming star Sirius. When the helical rising of Sirius occurs in July some trees will gain strength from his heat, while others wither in his heat. As Orion's hunting dog he pursues the Hare constellation.

This Sirius rite focuses on the Egyptian (Sothis) and the Persian/Vedic form (Tishtrya/Tir). Tishtrya is the Persian angel (Yazad) of the star Sirius. Tishtrya also presides over the fourth month and the thirteenth day of each month. Sirius also directs the rain; in the rite here included is an abridged version of this hymn. It covers the Tir story from the: helical rising of Sirius, bringer of rain, who flies like an arrow, his manifestation as a young man, a bull and a white horse, his battle against drought, and bringing fertility and rain onto the land.

The name of the Persian god/angel Tir means an *'arrow'* (modern day interpretations include bullet too). The Nordic Tyr, in runic language has the actual letter T shaped like an arrow head/spearhead, hence, it could mean arrow or spear, as well as victory.

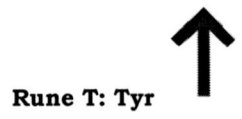

Rune T: Tyr ↑

Both these deities have sky god connections and are also warrior gods. The Tishtrya hymn also mentions arrows being fired.

Furthermore Tishtrya relates to the Babylonian god Ninurta who is the star Sirius. The star Sirius in Babylonian and Sumerian hymns is referred to as *'Arrow'* and *'Arrow star'*.[1]

The arrow link continues as there is also the Persian legend of Arash-Kamangir (the bowman) who fires an arrow to mark the borders of ancient Persia and is still celebrated as part of the Tir

Persian festival (Tigran: Summer Solstice). Arash means bright and shining, and Kamangir in means one who gets the arch, Kaman means bow. Arash was the Persian hero who sacrificed his life to preserve the borders of Iran. The legend of Arash-Kamangir and the arrow is still alive now, as in 1980 during the Iraq invasion of Iran, the Iranian Air Force led a mission codenamed 'Operation Kaman 99' where up to 140 fighter planes retaliated against Iraq *'likes arrows to mark the borders of modern Iran',* even though nearly half died heroically in the mission, they halted Iraq gaining air superiority and stopped their advance. This is a good example of how aerial and stellar legends and myths can inspire and influence us even in this modern era. NASA's Apollo missions and India's Agni space programme are other examples of myths inspiring contemporary people when naming important projects and events.

It should also be noted Mithra as the bowman opens the way to Tir the arrow. The water connection of Sothis and Tir is equally interesting. The heliacal rising of Sirius hails Tir as the bringer of rain in Persia and denotes Sothis as the bringer of floods in Egypt. The Persian Tir and the Nordic Tyr seem to be linked and have some interesting similarities. Canis Major the Great Dog of the sky perhaps acts as a celestial *'man's best friend';* a stellar guardian deity of our solar system!

Sirius is the sun behind the sun. In the heat of the *'dog days'* the extent of the *'dual'* influence of this star becomes most manifest, as the bringer of extensive heat and also rain/floods to quench the heat; the ultimate double-edged sword.

If you are interested in making a talisman of Sothis and Procyon, see the Invocations of the Greater & Lesser Dog stars in *Celestial Magic: Principles and Practises of the Talismanic* Art by Nigel Jackson. [2]

All of this information is just the tip of a very interesting iceberg. This rite aims to shed some light onto these mysteries; an intent of this rite could be to receive oracular wisdom from Sirius.

SIRIUS RITE

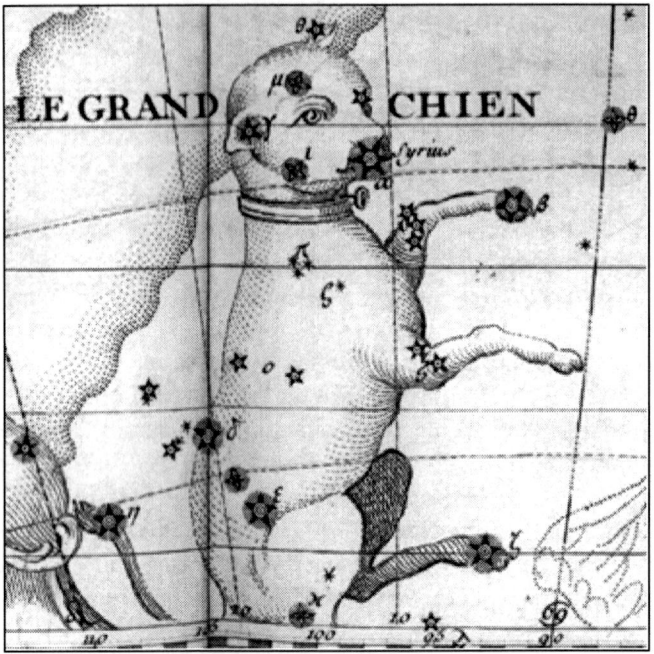

ATLAS CÉLESTE DE FLAMSTÉED

Altar Set up:

- ⊕ Candles or tea lights lit and place on altar in shape of constellation Canis Major, with a larger candle (or one with a different colour) to represent Sirius.
- ⊕ Altar to contain a large chalice full of water which is to be sprinkled on all.
- ⊕ Tektite or Moldavite (meteorite) stone.
- ⊕ Incense and incense burner.
- ⊕ Offerings: a plate of summer fruits, bread, meat. A chalice of wine and a chalice of milk.
- ⊕ Sistrum.
- ⊕ Altar cloth to have stars on it.
- ⊕ Rune letter T (Tyr).
- ⊕ If possible the rite is to be done at a location near water, for example a river, lake, or sea. If indoor play music (an appropriate piece would contain sounds of water or rain fall or use a rain stick).

Participants: Seven Mystes to volunteer, each to read their section. If this is a solo working rather than a group rite then all the parts are read by the one person. In case of groups working roles should be divided, ideally at least seven participants, if less then doubling up of roles is necessary.

AN EXAMPLE OF AN ALTAR TO CANIS MAJOR, LARGER RED CANDLE REPRESENTS SIRIUS (PHOTO BY P. NABARZ).

Opening:

The standard opening mentioned in the chapter *'opening and closing of rites'* is used here, **Mystes 1** reads the Orphic hymn to the stars, Followed by:

Mystes 2:

> "I invoke Sothis, Goddess of the star Sirius. And even when the Star of Knephhas has brought the summer round, and the Nile rises fast and full along the thirsty ground, you bless us. Yet are you two stars, Twin Beings. When Zulamith the Bold and Salami the Fair were building the Milky Way, they were separated for a thousand years as they toiled. When the road was finished, they were united:
> 'Straight rushed into each other's arms
> And melted into one:
> So they become the brightest star
> In heaven's high arch that dwelt –
> Great Sirius, the mighty Sun
> Beneath Orion's belt.'" [3]

Mystes 3:

"I am she that is the natural mother of all things, mistresses and governesses of all the Elements, the initial progeny of worlds, chief of powers divine, Queen of heaven! the principal of the Gods celestial, the light of the goddesses: at my will the planets of the air, the wholesome winds of the Seas, and the silences of hell be disposed; my name, my divinity is adored throughout all the world in diverse manners, in variable customs and in many names, for the Phrygians call me the mother of the Gods: the Athenians, Minerva: the Cyprians, Venus: the Candians, Diana: the Sicilians Proserpina: the Eleusians, Ceres: some Juno, other Bellona, other Hecate: and principally the Ethiopians which dwell in the Orient, and the Egyptians which are excellent in all kind of ancient doctrine, and by their proper ceremonies accustom to worship me, do call me Queen Isis."[4]

Mystes 4:

Tishtar (Tir) Yasht (Zoroastrian Hymn to the Star Sirius):[5]

"Unto Tishtrya, the bright and glorious star, and unto the powerful. We worship the Tishtrya, whereby he protects the Moon, the dwelling, the food, when my glorious stars come along and impart their gifts to men. We will sacrifice unto the star Tishtrya, that gives the fields their share of waters."

Mystes 5:

"We offer up libations unto Tishtrya, the bright and glorious star, that gives happy dwelling and good dwelling; the white, shining, seen afar, and piercing; the health-bringing, loud-snorting, and high, piercing from afar with its shining, undefiled rays; and unto the waters of the wide sea and the species of the Bull."

Mystes 6:

"For his brightness and glory, I will offer unto him a sacrifice worth being heard, namely, unto the star Tishtrya. Unto Tishtrya, the bright and glorious star, we offer up the libations, the Haoma and meat, the baresma, the wisdom of the tongue, the holy spells, the speech, the deeds, the libations, and the rightly-spoken words.
We sacrifice unto Tishtrya, the bright and glorious star, who is the seed of the waters, powerful, tall, and strong, whose light goes afar; powerful and highly working, through whom the brightness and the seed of the waters come from the high Apam Napat.
For his brightness and glory, I will offer him a sacrifice worth being heard...."

Mystes 7:

"We sacrifice unto Tishtrya, the bright and glorious star; for whom long flocks and herds and men, looking forward for him and deceived in their hope: When shall we see him rise up, the bright and glorious star Tishtrya? When will the springs run with waves as thick as a horse's size and still thicker? Or will they never come?

For his brightness and glory, I will offer him a sacrifice worth being heard...."

Mystes 1:

"We sacrifice unto Tishtrya, the bright and glorious star; who flies, towards the sea, as swiftly as the arrow darted through the heavenly space, which Erekhsha, the swift archer, the Arya amongst the Aryas whose arrow was the swiftest, shot from Mount to Mount.

For Ahura Mazda gave him assistance; so did the waters and the plants; and Mithra, the lord of wide pastures, opened a wide way unto him.

For his brightness and glory, I will offer him a sacrifice worth being heard....

We sacrifice unto Tishtrya, the bright and glorious star, that afflicts the Pairikas, that vexes the Pairikas, who, in the shape of worm-stars, fly between the earth and the heavens, in the sea, the powerful sea, the large-sized, deep sea of salt waters. He goes to its lake in the shape of a horse, in a holy shape; and down there he makes the waters boil over, and the winds flow above powerfully all around.

Those waters flow down to the seven continents of the earth, and when he has arrived down there, he stands beautiful, spreading ease and joy on the fertile countries

(thinking to himself): How shall the countries of the Aryas grow fertile?"

Mystes 2:

"If men would worship me with a sacrifice in which I were invoked by my own name, as they worship the other Yazatas with sacrifices in which they are invoked by their own names, then I should have come to the faithful at the appointed time; I should have come in the appointed time of my beautiful, immortal life, should it be one night, or two nights, or fifty, or a hundred nights.

We sacrifice unto the rains of Tishtrya. We sacrifice unto the first star; we sacrifice unto the rains of the first star, whose eye-sight is sound.

For ten nights, Tishtrya, the bright and glorious star, mingles his shape with light, moving in the shape of a man of fifteen years of age, bright, with clear eyes, tall, full of strength, strong, and clever.

*He is active as the first man was; he goes on with the strength of the first man; he has the virility of the first man.
Here he calls for people to assemble, here he asks, saying:
Who now will offer me the libations with the Haoma and the holy meat? To whom shall I give wealth of healthy children, a troop of healthy children, and the purification of his own soul?"*

Mystes 3:

*"The next ten nights the bright and glorious Tishtrya mingles his shape with light, moving in the shape of a golden-horned bull.
Here he calls for people to assemble, here he asks, saying:
Who now will offer me the libations with the Haoma and the holy meat? To whom shall I give wealth of oxen, a herd of oxen, and the purification of his own soul?
The next ten nights, the bright and glorious Tishtrya mingles his shape with light, moving in the shape of a white, beautiful horse, with golden ears and a golden caparison.
Here he calls for people to assemble, here he asks, saying:
Who now will offer me the libations with the Haoma and the holy meat?
To whom shall I give wealth of horses, a troop of horses, and the purification of his own soul?
Then, the bright and glorious Tishtrya goes down to the sea in the shape of a white, beautiful horse, with golden ears and a golden caparison.
But there rushes down to meet him the Daeva Apaosha (Drought), in the shape of a dark horse, black with black ears, black with a black back, black with a black tail, stamped with brands of terror.
They meet together, hoof against hoof, the bright and glorious Tishtrya and the Daeva Apaosha. They fight together for three days and three nights.
And then the Daeva Apaosha proves stronger than the bright and glorious Tishtrya, he overcomes him."*

Mystes 4:

*"And Tishtrya flees from the sea. He cries out in woe and distress, the bright and glorious Tishtrya: 'Woe is me, O Ahura Mazda! I am in distress, O Waters and Plants! O Fate
Men do not worship me with a sacrifice in which I am invoked by my own name, as they worship the other Yazatas with sacrifices in which they are invoked by their own names.
If men had worshipped me with a sacrifice in which I had been invoked by my own name, as they worship the other Yazatas with sacrifices in which they are invoked by their own names, I should have taken to me the strength of ten horses, the strength of ten camels, the strength of ten bulls, the strength of ten mountains, the strength of ten rivers.
Then I, Ahura Mazda, offer up to the bright and glorious Tishtrya a sacrifice in which he is invoked by his own name,*

and I bring him the strength of ten horses, the strength of ten camels, the strength of ten bulls, the strength of ten mountains, the strength of ten rivers.'"

Mystes 5:

"Then, the bright and glorious Tishtrya goes down to the sea in the shape of a white, beautiful horse, with golden ears and golden caparison.
But there rushes down to meet him the Daeva Apaosha (Drought) in the shape of a dark horse, black with black ears, black with a black back, black with a black tail, stamped with brands of terror.
They meet together, hoof against hoof, the bright and glorious Tishtrya, and the Daeva Apaosha; they fight together, till the time of noon. Then the bright and glorious Tishtrya proves stronger than the Daeva Apaosha, he overcomes him.
Then he goes from the sea 'Hail!' cries the bright and glorious Tishtrya.
Hail unto me, O Ahura Mazda! Hail unto you, O waters and plants! Hail, O Law of the worshippers! Hail will it be unto you, O lands! The life of the waters will flow down unrestrained to the big-seeded corn fields, to the small-seeded pasture-fields, and to the whole of the material world!
Then the bright and glorious Tishtrya goes back down to the sea, in the shape of a white, beautiful horse, with golden ears and a golden caparison.
He makes the sea boil up and down; he makes the sea stream this and that way; he makes the sea flow this and that way: all the shores of the sea are boiling over, all the middle of it is boiling over."

Mystes 6:

"And the bright and glorious Tishtrya rises up from the sea the bright and glorious Satavaesa rises up from the sea and vapours rise up above Mount that stands in the middle of the sea.
Then the vapours push forward, in the regular shape of clouds; they go following the wind, along the ways which Haoma traverses, the increaser of the world. Behind him travels the mighty wind, made by Mazda, and the rain, and the cloud, and the sleet, down to the several places, down to the fields, down to the seven continent of the earth.
Apam Napat, divides the waters amongst the countries in the material world, in company with the mighty wind, the Glory, made by the waters.
We sacrifice unto Tishtrya, the bright and glorious star, who from the shining east, moves along his long winding course, along the path made by the gods, along the way appointed for him the watery way."

Mystes 7:

"We sacrifice unto Tishtrya, the bright and glorious star, whose rising is watched by men who live on the fruits of the year, by the chiefs of deep understanding; by the wild beasts in the mountains, by the tame beasts that run in the plains; they watch him, as he comes up to the country for a bad year, or for a good year, (thinking in themselves): How shall the Aryan countries be fertile?

For his brightness and glory, I will offer him a sacrifice worth being heard....

We sacrifice unto Tishtrya, the bright and glorious star, swift-flying and swift-moving, who flies towards the sea, as swiftly as the arrow darted through the heavenly space, which Erekhsha, the swift archer, the Arya amongst the Aryas whose arrow was the swiftest, shot from Mount to Mount.

Ahura Mazda gave him assistance, and the Amesha-Spentas and Mithra, the lord of wide pastures, pointed him the way: behind him went the tall Ashish Vanguhi and Parendi on her light chariot:

always till, in his course, he reached Mount Hvanvant on the shining waters.

For his brightness and glory, I will offer him a sacrifice worth being heard..."

Mystes 1:

"We sacrifice unto Tishtrya, the bright and glorious star, who afflicts the Pairikas, who destroys the Pairikas, that Angra Mainyus flung to stop all the stars that have in them the seed of the waters.

Tishtrya afflicts them, he blows them away from the sea Vouru-Kasha; then the wind blows the clouds forward, bearing the waters of fertility, so that the friendly showers spread wide over, they spread helpingly and friendly over the seven continents.

For his brightness and glory, I will offer him a sacrifice worth being heard....

We sacrifice unto Tishtrya, the bright and glorious star, for who long the standing waters, and the running spring-waters, the stream-waters, and the rain-waters:

When will the bright and glorious Tishtrya rise up for us? When will the springs with a flow and overflow of waters, thick as a horse's shoulder, run to the beautiful places and fields, and to the pastures, even to the roots of the plants, that they may grow with a powerful growth?

For his brightness and glory, I will offer him a sacrifice worth being heard..."

Mystes 2:

"We sacrifice unto Tishtrya, the bright and glorious star, who washes away all things of fear, who stunts the growth of all

and brings health to all these creations, being most beneficent, when he has been worshipped with a sacrifice and propitiated, rejoiced, and satisfied.
We will sacrifice unto Tishtrya, the bright and glorious star, whom has established as a lord and overseer above all stars,
We sacrifice unto Tishtrya, the bright and glorious star, to whom Ahura Mazda has given a thousand senses, and who is the most beneficent amongst the stars that have in them the seed of the waters:
Who moves in light with the stars that have in them the seed of the waters: he, from the sea Vouru-Kasha, the powerful sea, the large-sized, deep, and salt of waters, goes to all the lakes, and to all the beautiful caves, and to all the beautiful channels, in the shape of a white, beautiful horse, with golden ears and a golden caparison.
Then, the waters flow down from the sea, mother-like, friendly, and healing: he divides them amongst these countries, being most beneficent, when he has been worshipped with a sacrifice and propitiated rejoiced, and satisfied.....
We sacrifice unto Tishtrya, the bright and glorious star, for whom long all the creatures, those that live under the ground, and those that live above the ground; those that live in the waters, and those that live on dry land; those that fly, and those that run in the plains; and all those that live within this boundless and endless world of the Spirit.
We sacrifice unto Tishtrya, the bright and glorious star, the healthful, wise, happy, and powerful, who is the lord of a thousand boons, and grants many boons to that man who has pleased him, whether begging or not begging for them.
If the Aryan countries, would perform in honour of the bright and glorious Tishtrya the due sacrifice and invocation, just as that sacrifice and invocation ought to be performed in the perfection of holiness; never should a hostile horde enter these Aryan countries, nor any plague, nor leprosy, nor venomous plants, nor the chariot of a foe, nor the uplifted spear of a foe.
What is then, the sacrifice and invocation in honour of the bright and glorious Tishtrya, as it ought to be performed in the perfection of holiness?
Answered: Let the Aryan people bring libations unto him; let the Aryan people tie bundles of baresma for him; let the Aryan people cook for him a head of cattle, either white, or black, or of any other colour, but all of one and the same colour.
We bless the sacrifice and prayer, and the strength and vigour of Tishtrya, the bright and glorious star, and of the powerful Satavaesa, made by Mazda, who pushes waters forward.
Give unto us brightness and glory, ... give us the bright, all-happy, blissful abode of the holy Ones." [8]

- ⊕ Sit down to meditate for a while on what has been said, relevant music could be played to help with the meditation
- ⊕ Saying of thanks to spirits of the place.
- ⊕ Final thanks to Sirius.

The standard closing mentioned in the chapter *'opening and closing of rites'* is used here. *Mystes 1* recites the closing Orphic hymn to the stars. This is followed by having something to eat and drink. Then clear the space.

References.

1. *Astral Magic in Babylonia,* Reiner, Erica; 1995; in *Transactions of the American Philosophical Society*, New Series, Vol. 85.4:i-150. See pp19-20.
2. Appendix 7 Invocations of the Greater & Lesser Dog stars pages160-162 in *Celestial Magic: Principles and Practises of the Talismanic Art* by Nigel Jackson, Cap all Bann Publishing, 2003.
3. *Winter Star Rite* by Olivia Robertson, Fellowship of Isis.
4. *The Golden Ass* by Lucius Apuleius "Africanus", translated by William Adlington, 1566, Book 11.
5. *Tishtar Yasht (8), Avesta: Khorda Avesta* (Book of Common Prayer) Translation by James Darmesteter, from *Sacred Books of the East*, American Edition, 1898.

Further reading:

Issue 3 of The *Oracle* occult magazine (Autumn Equinox 2005) had a very interesting article on Sirius by Frater Indred and mentioned that the proper name of Sirius within Tyr constellation was Loki's brand. It was a two part article, followed in issue 4.

For looking at various hypotheses around the influence of Sirius:
The Sirius connection: Unlocking the Secrets of Ancient Egypt, Murry Hope, Element, 1996.
The Sirius Mystery: Conclusive New Evidence of Alien Influence on the Origins of Humankind in the Traditions of an African Tribe, Robert K.G. Temple, Century, 1998.

Notes:

Constellations Perseus & Andromeda

A Stellar Beltane Rite to constellations Perseus and Andromeda, star crossed lovers.

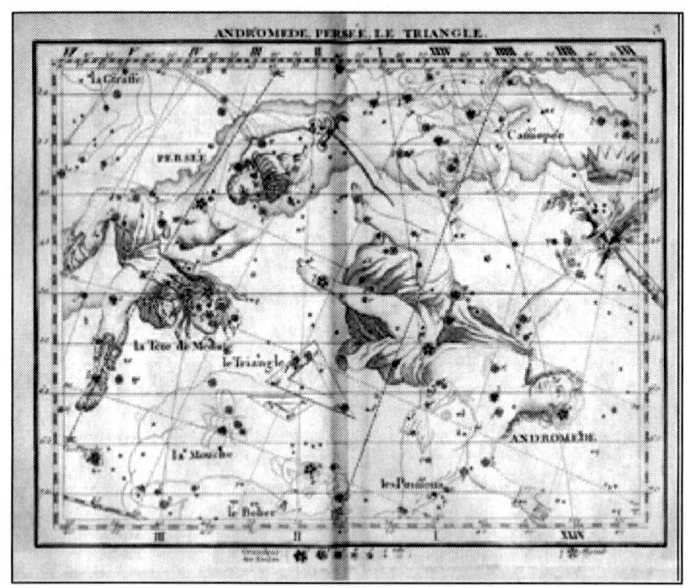

ATLAS CÉLESTE DE FLAMSTÉED

Introduction

"For I am divided for love's sake, for the chance of union."
—Nuit (*Liber AL*)

This is a story which involves six constellations, Pegasus, Cetus, Cassiopeia, Cepheus, Perseus and Andromeda. According to Aratus' *Phaenomena,* Queen Cassiopeia in Greek mythology was married to King Iasid Cepheus of Ethiopia and their daughter was Andromeda.

They were akin to Zeus as they descended from Io. One day Cassiopeia announced that she was more beautiful than the Aegean Sea nymphs the Nereids. The sea nymphs Doris and Panope on hearing this complained to the sea god Poseidon, who decided to avenge the insult by sending floods to Cepheus' kingdom, followed by sending the Cetus, a sea monster. To appease Poseidon and the sea monster, the court Oracles advised the king to sacrifice Andromeda to the monster. She was then chained to a rock on the cliffs by the sea. The hero Perseus was flying on Pegasus across the sky having killed Medusa already and was carrying her head in his bag, when he came across Andromeda chained to the rock. He immediately falls in love with her and asks for her hand in marriage, which she agrees. He also obtained Kings Cepheus permission, which was given if he could defeat the monster. Perseus accepted the challenge and flew on his horse Pegasus and attacked the monster. He succeeded in killing the monster by taking Medusa's head out of the bag and showing it to the sea monster. The monster upon looking on Medusa's head turns to stone. Perseus and Andromeda hence married and were given a kingdom of their own by Cepheus. Their first son was called Perses (Persian) and was said to be the ancestor of the Persians. When Andromeda and Perseus died they were placed among the stars, along with all the main characters of the story. The constellation Perseus is still defending Andromeda from constellation Cetus the leviathan of the sky. Perseus' horse constellation Pegasus flies close to the constellation Andromeda who appears chained with her arms stretched across. Andromeda's parents King Cepheus and Queen Cassiopeia are also constellations and both sit on their thrones near their daughter. However, Cassiopeia as part of the punishment for her insult to the sea nymphs is sometimes turned upside-down while in her throne in the sky. She can be easily spotted as her constellation is in shape of W or E. The Cepheus constellation is next to the Cassiopeia constellation. The Pegasus constellation can be spotted by locating the *'Square of Pegasus'* next to constellation Andromeda, they have a star in common. Pegasus was flying upside down in the night sky. In addition to flying Perseus, the Pegasus was according to Aratus' *Phaenomena* famed for stamping his hoof at the summit of Helicon and water emerged from where his foot had stricken the ground.

There are some beautiful modern poems which link with the Perseus current for example *Perseus - The Triumph of Wit Over Suffering* by Sylvia Plath (1932-1963), and *Perseus* by Robert Hayden (1913-1980) in addition to the poems included here.

PERSEUS AND ANDROMEDA RITE
(A TALE FOR LOVERS AT BELTANE)
OMNIA VINCIT AMOR - LOVE CONQUERS ALL THINGS.

The format of this rite is along the lines of a Bardic *Eisteddfod*, where great poems are recited. The rite here is set up as a group ceremony; however, it can be adapted for a couple or solo working.

Set up
- Location: a place with good visibility of the stars.
- Central fire lit but kept to a size not to affect the night vision too much.
- Time is determined using a Star-globe or Star-chart ensuring visibility of Perseus and Andromeda constellations.
- Clothing: sensible outdoor clothing & footwear.
- Food and drink to share.

The standard opening mentioned in the chapter *'opening and closing of rites'* is used here.

After the opening *Soror 1* recites the following while others listen and mediate on the tale.

A Tale of lovers for Beltane, Perseus and Andromeda Rite
From *Metamorphoses* by Ovid Book IV which can viewed as the *'Charge of Perseus and Andromeda'*.

"Andromeda rescued from the Sea Monster:
Now Aeolus had with strong chains confined,
And deep imprisoned every blustering wind,
The rising Phosper with a purple light
Did sluggish mortals to new toils invite.
His feet again the valiant Perseus plumes,
And his keen sabre in his hand resumes:
Then nobly spurns the ground, and upwards springs,
And cuts the liquid air with sounding wings.
O'er various seas, and various lands he past,
Until Aethiopia's shore appeared at last.
Andromeda was there, doomed to atone
By her own ruin follies not her own:
And if injustice in a God can be,
Such was the Libyan God's unjust decree.
Chained to a rock she stood; young Perseus stayed
His rapid flight, to view the beauteous maid.

So sweet her frame, so exquisitely fine,
She seemed a statue by a hand divine,
Had not the wind her waving tresses showed,
And down her cheeks the melting sorrows flowed.
Her faultless form the hero's bosom fires;
The more he looks, the more he still admires.
The' admirer almost had forgot to fly,
And swift descended fluttering from on high.
O! Virgin, worthy no such chains to prove,
But pleasing chains in the soft folds of love;
And give a true rehearsal of thy woes.
A quick reply her bashfulness refused,
To the free converse of a man unused.
Her rising blushes had concealment found
From her spread hands, but that her hands were bound.
She acted to her full extent of power,
And bathed her face with a fresh, silent shower.
But by degrees in innocence grown bold,
Her name, her country, and her birth she told:
And how she suffered for her mother's pride,
Who with the Nereids once in beauty vied.
Part yet untold, the seas began to roar,
And mounting billows tumbled to the shore.
Above the waves a monster raised his head,
His body o'er the deep was widely spread:
Onward he flounced; aloud the virgin cries;
Each parent to her shrieks in shrieks replies:
But she had deepest cause to rend the skies.
Weeping, to her they cling; no sign appears
Of help, they only lend their helpless tears.
Too long you vent your sorrows, Perseus said,
Short is the hour, and swift the time of aid,
In me the son of thundering Jove behold,
Got in a kindly shower of fruitful gold.
Medusa's snaky head is now my prey,
And thro' the clouds I boldly wing my way.
If such desert be worthy of esteem,
And, if your daughter I from death redeem,
Shall she be mine? Shall it not then be thought,
A bride, so lovely, was too cheaply bought?
For her my arms I willingly employ,
If I may beauties, which I save, enjoy.
The parents eagerly the terms embrace:
For who would slight such terms in such a case?
Nor her alone they promise, but beside,
The dowry of a kingdom with the bride.
As well-rigged galleys, which slaves, sweating, row,
With their sharp beaks the whitened ocean plough;
So when the monster moved, still at his back
The furrowed waters left a foamy track.
Now to the rock he was advanced so nigh,

Whirled from a sling a stone the space would fly.
Then bounding, upwards the brave Perseus sprung,
And in mid air on hovering pinions hung.
His shadow quickly floated on the main;
The monster could not his wild rage restrain,
But at the floating shadow leaped in vain.
As when Jove's bird, a speckled serpent spies,
Which in the shine of Phoebus basking lies,
Unseen, he souses down, and bears away,
Trussed from behind, the vainly-hissing prey.
To writhe his neck the labour naught avails,
Too deep the imperial talons pierce his scales.
Thus the winged hero now descends, now soars,
And at his pleasure the vast monster gores.
Full in his back, swift stooping from above,
The crooked sabre to its hilt he drove.
The monster raged, impatient of the pain,
First bounded high, and then sunk low again.
Now, like a savage boar, when chafed with wounds,
And bayed with opening mouths of hungry hounds,
He on the foe turns with collected might,
Who still eludes him with an airy flight;
And wheeling round, the scaly armour tries
Of his thick sides; his thinner tall now plies:
'Till from repeated strokes out gushed a flood,
And the waves reddened with the streaming blood.
At last the dropping wings, be foamed all over,
With flaggy heaviness their master bore:
A rock he spied, whose humble head was low,
Bare at an ebb, but covered at a flow.
A ridge hold, he, thither flying, gained,
And with one hand his bending weight sustained;
With the' other, vigorous blows he dealt around,
And the home-thrusts the expiring monster owned.
In deafening shouts the glad applauses rise,
And peal on peal runs rattling thro' the skies."[1]

"For I am divided for love's sake, for the chance of union."
– Nuit (Liber Al)

[Notes: The group at this stage is divided into two groups: men and women. Each group is standing on either side of the fire. After looking at the constellations the following poems are recited, the Fraters calling on Andromeda, the Sorors calling on Perseus. Men are calling on their stellar lover Andromeda, while women are calling on their stellar lover Perseus, inviting them to the circle.]

***Frater 1* recites:**

Andromeda (by Thomas Bailey Aldrich 1836 – 1907)
> "The smooth-worn coin and threadbare classic phrase
> Of Grecian myths that did beguile my youth,
> Beguile me not as in the olden days:
> I think more grief and beauty dwell with truth.
> Andromeda, in fetters by the sea,
> Star-pale with anguish till young Perseus came,
> Less moves me with her suffering than she,
> The slim girl figure fettered to dark shame,
> That nightly haunts the park, there, like a shade,
> Trailing her wretchedness from street to street.
> See where she passes -- neither wife nor maid;
> How all mere fiction crumbles at her feet!
> Here is woe's self, and not the mask of woe:
> A legend's shadow shall not move you so! "[2]

***Soror 1* recites:**
> "The saviour-youth the royal pair confess,
> And with heaved hands their daughter's bridegroom bless.
> The beauteous bride moves on, now loosed from chains,
> The cause, and sweet reward of all the hero's pains,
> Mean-time, on shore triumphant Perseus stood,
> And purged his hands, smeared with the monster's blood:
> Then in the windings of a sandy bed
> Composed Medusa's execrable head.
> But to prevent the roughness, leafs he threw,
> And young, green twigs, which soft in waters grew,
> There soft, and full of sap; but here, when laid,
> Touched by the head, that softness soon decayed.
> The wonted flexibility quite gone,
> The tender scions hardened into stone.
> Fresh, juicy twigs, surprised, the Nereid's brought,
> Fresh, juicy twigs the same contagion caught.
> The nymphs the petrifying seeds still keep,
> And propagate the wonder thro' the deep.
> The pliant sprays of coral yet declare
> Their stiffening Nature, when exposed to air.
> Those sprays, which did, like bending osiers, move,
> Snatched from their element, obdurate prove,
> And shrubs beneath the waves grow stones above."[1]

***Frater 2* recites:**

Andromeda (by Gerard Manley Hopkins 1844-1889)
> "Now Time's Andromeda on this rock rude,
> With not her either beauty's equal or
> Her injury's, looks off by both horns of shore,
> Her flower, her piece of being, doomed dragon's food.
> Time past she has been attempted and pursued

*By many blows and banes; but now hears roar
A wilder beast from West than all were, more
Rife in her wrongs, more lawless, and more lewd.
Her Perseus linger and leave her to her extremes?
Pillowy air he treads a time and hangs
His thoughts on her, forsaken that she seems,
All while her patience, morselled into pangs,
Mounts; then to alight disarming, no one dreams,
With Gorgon's gear and barebill, thongs and fangs."*[3]

Soror 2 recites:

*"The great immortals grateful Perseus praised,
And to three Powers three turf altars raised.
To Hermes this; and that he did assign
To Pallas: the mid honours, Jove, were thine,
He hastes for Pallas a white cow to cull,
A calf for Hermes, but for Jove a bull.
Then seized the prize of his victorious fight,
Andromeda, and claimed the nuptial rite.
Andromeda alone he greatly sought,
The dowry kingdom was not worth his thought.
Pleased Hymen now his golden torch displays;
With rich oblations fragrant altars blaze,
Sweet wreaths of choicest flowers are hung on high,
And cloudless pleasure smiles in every eye.
The melting music melting thoughts inspires,
And warbling songsters aid the warbling lyres.
The palace opens wide in pompous state,
And by his peers surrounded, Cepheus sate.
A feast was served, fit for a king to give,
And fit for God-like heroes to receive.
The banquet ended, the gay, cheerful bowl
Moved round, and brightened, and enlarged each soul.
Then Perseus asked, what customs there obtained,
And by what laws the people were restrained.
Which told; the teller a like freedom takes,
And to the warrior his petition makes,
To know, what arts had won Medusa's snakes."*[1]

- ⊕ The spark is kindled by the opposite gender calling on their constellation. Next men to *'draw down'* Perseus and women to *'draw down'* Andromeda to themselves.
- ⊕ Use music, chant, dance and any other technique, (if it feels appropriate) to infuse yourself with the Perseus and Andromeda current and a reach a trance state. The goal is at least one person in each group will be giving an Oracle of Perseus and Andromeda in turn. If more than one person in the group is in trance, then continue

- to give Oracles in turn, until all have spoken. The Oracle may be interactive between Perseus and Andromeda, as they speak to each other as well as to the gathering.
- If it feels appropriate perhaps each group will make a sigil representing their constellations. After the Oracles have been given the two sigils are united and tied together with a string and then if possible placed in the river (symbolic Milky Way) to float away to cosmic bliss. If you are not near a river during the rite, hold on to the sigil and float it later when you are able to get to a river or lake or sea.
- The two groups become one circle again and a simple circle dance helps to finish the unity of the two.
- Sit down to meditate for a while on what has been said, some relevant music could be played to help with the meditation.
- Saying of thanks to spirits of the place.
- Final thanks to Cepheus, Cassiopeia, Perseus, Andromeda, Cetus and Pegasus.

The standard closing mentioned in the chapter *'opening and closing of rites'* is used here. This is followed by having something to eat and drink. Then clear the space.

References
1. The *Metamorphoses* of Ovid translated into English verse under the direction of Sir Samuel Garth by John Dryden, Alexander Pope, Joseph Addison, William Congreve and other eminent hands, 1717.
Another translation available is
The Metamorphoses of Ovid Vol. I, Books I-VII Translator: Henry Thomas Riley, 1893.
Other translations include: May M. Innes, Penguin Classics (1955, New Edition 2002) and David Raeburn translation, Penguin Classics; New Ed edition (2004).
2. *Andromeda* by Thomas Bailey Aldrich (1836–1907).
3. *Andromeda* by Gerard Manley Hopkins (1844-1889).

Further reading:
The Metamorphoses of Ovid translated by M. Innes, Penguin Classics (1955, New Edition 2002)
Star Myths of the Greeks and Romans: A Sourcebook, by Theony Condos, Phanes Press, U.S, 1997.
Sun, Moon & Stars by Sheena McGrath, Capall Bann, 2005.

Notes:

THE MOON

FULL MOON RISING OVER STONEHENGE, PHOTO BY P. NABARZ

INTRODUCTION

*"To behold the wandering Moon,
Riding near her highest noon,
Like one that had been led astray
Through the Heavens wide pathless way."*
                                        -Milton II Penseroso.

Moon deities feature in almost all ancient religions, in some cultures the moon is seen as a goddess and in some as a god. Moon Gods include the Phrygian Men, the Egyptian Thoth, the Sumerian Sin, the Shinto Tsukiyomi, the Hindu Chandra, and the Norse Mani. Moon Goddesses include the Persian Mah, the Roman Diana and Luna, the Greek Selene and Artemis to name a few.

There has been a great deal written about working with the moon in the last 50 years by modern pagans, its central role in neo-paganism and 20th century religion Wicca is well documented by a number of books on the subject. The technique of drawing down the moon is a major part of Wicca, as this is an introductory book it is prudent to cover this first. Readers familiar with drawing dawn the moon technique and Wicca may want to skip the next couple of pages while this is reviewed for the benefit of those who may not be familiar with it. There are several different versions of this method in Wicca, one adaptation of the approach from the Gardnerian Book of Shadows in brief is:

The High Priestess stands in front of Altar which is in the North and faces south. She stands in Goddess position (arms crossed as Osiris). High Priest/Magus, kneels in front of her and draws a pentacle on her body with a Phallus-headed Wand, and invokes:

> 'I Invoke and beseech Thee, O mighty Mother of all life and fertility. By seed and root, by stem and bud, by leaf and flower and fruit, by Life and Love, do I invoke Thee to descend into the body of thy servant and High Priestess [name]'

The Moon having been drawn down, the Magus and other men give the five-fold kiss:

> (kissing feet)
> 'Blessed be thy feet, that have brought thee in these ways;'
> (kissing knees)
> 'Blessed be thy knees, that shall kneel at the sacred altar;'
> (kissing womb)
> 'Blessed be thy womb, without which we would not be;'
> (kissing breasts)
> 'Blessed be thy breasts, formed in beauty and in strength;'
> (kissing lips)
> 'Blessed be thy lips, that shall speak the sacred names.'

Women all bow.

Next the Charge of the Goddess is recited:

> Magus/High Priest: 'Listen to the words of the Great mother, who was of old also called among men, Artemis, Astarte, Anahita, Dione, Melusine, Aphrodite, Ceridwen, Diana, Arianrhod, Bride, (insert your preferred goddesses here) and by many other names.'

> High Priestess: 'At mine Altars the youth of Lacedaemon in Sparta made due sacrifice. Whenever ye have need of anything, once in the month, and better it be when the moon is full. Then ye shall assemble in some secret place and adore the spirit of Me who am Queen of all Witcheries. There ye shall assemble, ye who are fain to learn all sorcery, yet who have not won its deepest secrets. To these will I teach things that are yet unknown. And ye shall be free from slavery, and as a sign that ye be really free, ye shall be naked in your rites, and ye shall dance, sing, feast, make music, and love, all in my praise. For

mine is the ecstasy of the Spirit, and mine is also joy on earth. For my Law is Love unto all beings. Keep pure your highest ideals. Strive ever towards it. Let naught stop you or turn you aside. For mine is the secret which opens upon the door of youth; and mine is the cup of the Wine of Life: and the Cauldron of Ceridwen, which is the Holy Grail of Immortality. I am the Gracious Goddess who gives the gift of Joy unto the heart of Man. Upon Earth I give the knowledge of the Spirit Eternal, and beyond death I give peace and freedom, and reunion with those who have gone before. Nor do I demand aught in sacrifice, for behold, I am the Mother of all things, and my love is poured out upon earth.'
Magus/High Priest: 'Hear ye the words of the Star Goddess, She in the dust of whose feet are the hosts of Heaven, whose body encircleth the universe.'

High Priestess: 'I who am the beauty of the green earth; and the White Moon amongst the Stars; and the mystery of the Waters; and the desire of the heart of man. I call unto thy soul: arise and come unto me. For I am the Soul of nature who giveth life to the Universe; From me all things proceed; and unto me, all things must return. Beloved of the Gods and men, thine inmost divine self shall be enfolded in the raptures of the infinite. Let my worship be within the heart that rejoiceth, for behold: all acts of love and pleasure are my rituals; and therefore let there be Beauty and Strength, Power and Compassion, Honour and Humility, Mirth and reverence within you. And thou who thinkest to seek me, know that thy seeking and yearning shall avail thee not unless thou know the mystery, that if that which thou seekest thou findest not within thee, thou wilt never find it without thee, for behold; I have been with thee from the beginning, and I am that which is attained at the end of desire.'[2]

In this Wiccan method which uses male/female polarity, the High Priest draws down the moon onto the High Priestess, who then gives voice to the Moon Goddess. During the Charge of the Goddesses, in a way a plethora of goddesses are being channelled through the priestess, not just the moon, the moon acts as the starting point, and the initial focus. The priestess following from being the Moon Goddess, then channels the Earth Goddess too, the Great Mother. The next stage is clearly marked by High Priest/Magus saying:

"Hear ye the words of the Star Goddess, She in the dust of whose feet are the hosts of Heaven, whose body encircleth the universe."

The High Priestess now channels the Star Goddess, in her myriad of forms, for example the Egyptian star goddess Nuit. This is perhaps the climax of the oracle, giving voice to star goddess Nuit. How can we be certain it is Egyptian star goddess Nuit? The answer lies in those parts of the Wiccan drawing down the moon and *'Charge of the Goddess'* that appear to be based partly on the *Gnostic Mass* and *Book of the Law* by Aleister Crowley. Specifically in the section in the *Ceremony of the Opening of the Veil* in the *Gnostic Mass* reads:

> *The Priest:*
> *"O circle of Stars whereof our Father is but the younger brother, marvel beyond imagination, soul of infinite space, before whom Time is Ashamed, the mind bewildered, and the understanding dark, not unto Thee may we attain, unless Thine image be Love. Therefore by seed and root and stem and bud and leaf and flower and fruit do we invoke Thee."*[3]

Further more in *Book of the Law* (Liber AL vel Legis) verse 27 reads:

> *"Then the priest answered & said unto the Queen of Space, kissing her lovely brows, and the dew of her light bathing his whole body in a sweet-smelling perfume of sweat: O Nuit, continuous one of Heaven, let it be ever thus; that men speak not of Thee as One but as None; and let them speak not of thee at all, since thou art continuous!"*[4]

The most moving lines of chapter 1 of *Liber AL* should also be examined here, starting from verse 61 reads:

> *"But to love me is better than all things; if under the night-stars in the desert thou presently burnest mine incense before me, invoking me with a pure heart, and the serpent flame therein, thou shalt come a little to lie in my bosom. For one kiss wilt thou then be willing to give all; but whoso gives one particle of dust shall lose all in that hour. Ye shall gather goods and store of women and spices; ye shall wear rich jewels; ye shall exceed the nations of the earth in splendour and pride; but always in the love of me, and so shall ye come to my joy. I charge you earnestly to come before me in a single robe, and covered with a rich head-dress. I love you! I yearn to you! Pale or purple, veiled or voluptuous, I who am all pleasure and purple, and drunkenness of the innermost sense, desire you. Put on the wings, and arouse the coiled splendour within you: come unto me! To me! To me! Sing the rapturous love-song unto me! Burn to me perfumes! Wear to me jewels! Drink to me, for I love you! I love you. I am the blue-lidded daughter of sunset; I am the naked brilliance of the voluptuous night-sky. To me! To me!!"*[4]

To summarise, Stellar deities and workings are a major part of neo-paganism, be it Wicca or Thelema, or many other branches of modern paganism. The Queen of Space, Nuit, and Arianrhod are just some of the names used. The neo-pagan drawing down the moon rite, begins with the connecting to a lunar goddess and ends with a dialogue with the Queen of Space.

It should also be noted in drawing down the sun in Wicca the priest stands and gives voice to the gods while the priestess draws the sun into him and gives him the fivefold kiss (as in the drawing down the moon version).

The above basic introduction looks at the well known drawing down the moon technique as covered in Wicca and looks at the Gnostic Mass. As effective and cosmic as this approach is for couples and a group, a different approach is needed for solo practitioners.

In the lunar rite described below another approach is suggested here, which is drawing down the moon into a chalice/ bowl while reciting ancient hymns to the moon and then drinking the water (or mead), hence taking moon energy inside that way (symbolically or literally depending on your views). It can be done as a solo, couple or group. It is also not gender specific and it can easily be done outdoor in cold winter nights.

Specific ritual workings set up with the aim of making contact with different aspect of the moon in the lunar calendar can be done by working with the themes of the moon names. There are many full moon naming conventions for referring to different moon/full moons in the wheel of the year from different cultures and countries. One version that is useful and combines several different naming conventions is starting from September's full moon is: Harvest Moon, Hunters Moon, Blood Moon (or Beaver Moon), Long Night Moon, Ice Moon, Snow Moon, Storm Moon, Seed Moon, Flower Moon, Rose Moon, Mead Moon, and Corn Moon. When an extra full moon occurs in a month this is the Blue Moon. The names help to tune into the major agricultural activity and seasonal current. These are precursors to the modern biodynamic techniques in horticulture. The harvesting comes to an end in September, hence the Harvest Moon. Frequently when the Moon rises in October it can be appear red briefly (depending where you are) and the end of October is Samhain and killing of animals that could not survive the winter, and also an opportunity to hunt before winter. Hence, several factors result in the October full moon being called Hunters Moon. The rest of the names of the moons have folklore linked to it some more obvious that others, e.g. long winter night moon is December moon and Yule the longest night.

It is recommended to at least carry out a full year of lunar rites working with the moon at different times of the year. The naming convention does to a large extent depend where in the world you are based; therefore you may prefer to create your own system.

The moon as well as being worshipped, was seen to influence many events, and, moon omens are seen in many cultures. For example according to folk lore, a halo round the moon is said to indicate rain, and if stars are in the halo, the number of stars indicate number of days it would rain. An interesting lunar omen system was developed by Persian Zoroastrians called: *Persian Burj Nameh*: the book of omens from the moon.[5] Burj Nameh can also translate as *'book of the constellations'*. This is a Persian poem of 26 couplets in Persian lyrical rhyme and are part of the *'Parsee Revayats'* prose and poem collection, whose official title is *Revayet-i Darab Hormazdyar- Autograph of the compiler written 1679 AD*. It is uncertain how old Burj Nameh actually is; while it was written down in 1679 AD it is probably several centuries older. However, while this text is an important part of the Zoroastrian body of work, it is not seen as the words of the Prophet Zoroaster himself as stated in the *Gathas* texts. The couplets are saying what the appearance of the new moon portends in each of the Zodiac signs. The following is a combination of my translation and that of Louis H. Gray paper[5]. Also included is a new calligraphy of the Persian text. A similar approach was taken in my book *The Persian 'Mar Nameh': The Zoroastrian 'Book of the Snake' Omens and Calendar*. Both Burj Nameh and Mar Nameh are closely linked.

PERSIAN BURJ NAMEH:

BOOK OF OMENS FROM THE MOON

FULL MOON, PHOTO BY P. NABARZ.

*"In the name of kind and righteous God
By kindness of God who, provides man's daily portions.
I will tell what each new moon entails.*

*When you see the new moon seen in sign of Aries
Immediately look into a fire in that moment.
If in that month your work was better
Take that as symbol of your sprouted spring seed in your jar+*

*When you see the new moon in Taurus
Look upon a cow and this month would be better existence for you*

*When you see a new moon in Gemini
In that time look upon her shining face directly
Avoid looking at a blind person
And the month will be more beneficent for you.
When you see the new moon in the sign of Cancer
Listen to the news from your doctor.
In that moment look at a flowing river
And a good green pasture*

*When you see the new moon in sign of Leo
Set your gaze upon the sky
State your need to the pure God and*

Avoid seeing a children and women if feasible, o celebrated person.

*When you see the new moon in Virgo
listen to these wise words:
look not on a copper worker when smoke of smouldering rises
to avoid becoming sad.*

*Recite with sincerity the prayers to God
If you like happiness in that new moon*

*When you see the new moon in Libra
Look upon a mirror or golden surface
State your needs to the creator of the world
I will tell you what I can of the sign of Scorpio also*

*Look upon the coming days with kindness
Chivalrous person tradition is not blind or deaf
Don't gaze on forbidden objects
So that moons grace reaches you.*

*When you see the moon is in sign of Sagittarius
Look immediately upon silver and gold.
and avoid looking at face of a sick person
Be vigilant so that you will become happy*

*When you see the new moon in sign of Capricorn
Immediately recite three times the Ashim Ahu (Yasna xxvii 14) prayer and
Avoid looking at children and sick people
Otherwise you will be unhappy that month.*

*When you see the new moon in sign of Aquarius
Recite the prayer Ayta Ahu Vair (Yasna xxvii 13) and listen to its words
State your need to the mighty creator and
Avoid looking at women and children o famous one!*

*When you see the moon in sign of Pisces
Immediately look upon jewels and gems
Look upon them and be happy from then
be happy as no harm will come to you.*

*Likewise this way the snake is now,
the guardian is the creator."*

+ grain jar probably refers to the sprouting of grain for Spring Equinox (Nou Roz).

Persian Calligraphy Text of Burj Nameh

برج نامه

بنام ایزد مهربان دادگر

ز لطف خداوند روزی رسان	بگویم زهر ماه نو میتوان
زبرج حمل چو به بینی نو ماه	یکن اندر آن دم آتش نگاه
گران ماه کارت بود خوبتر	ز کشت ردان کنون در نگر
هم از تو رنگ بر به بینی گورا	گران ماه بهتر بود مرترا
چو در برج جوزا به بینی نو ماه	در آن وقت کن تو بر اهر نگاه
بپرهیز از کور و اورا مبین	گر باشدت آن ماه نیکو ترین
چو در برج خرچنگ بینی قمر	ز گفت حکیم این تو بشنو خبر
در آن دم نظر کن ب آب روان	گر سبزه را خوب یا او رودان
زبرج اسد چو به بینی نو ماه	تو بر آسمان کن زمانی نگاه

بخواه حاجت از پاک پروردگار	مبین کودک وزن توان نامدار
چو در برج خوشه به بینی تو دان	ز مضمون او بشنو من چنان
مبین تو جبان رود گر کس نزد و د	گر نعلین نکردی تو خود با وجود
بخوان ذکر یزدان بصدق درست	گر خوشنما کردی در آن ماه نوست
چو در برج میزان به بینی قمر	در آینه وزر در آ مزم نگر
بخواه حاجت از کردگار جهان	هم از برج عقرب بگویم توان
تو نیکو کار ایام بنیکو نظر	جوانمرد باش نه کور دنه کر
مبین چیز مکروه ای نامور	گر آن مه به نیکی رسد خود بر
چو در برج قوس اندر آید قمر	همانگه نگه کن ابا سیم و زر
مبین روی بیمار را آن زمان	بسپر هنر تا خود شوی شادمان

از برج جدی چو به بینی نو مه / اشیم اهو بر خوان همانگه سه ره

تو منگر ز بیمار و هم کودکان / گر باشی در آن مه مبینا دمان

چو دلو در بینی همی ماه نو / اینا اهو و پیر من خوان توانها شنو

بخواه حاجت از قادر کردگار / مبین کودک و زن توای نامدار

چو در برج ماهی به بینی تو ماه / به لعل و جواهر کن آنگه نگاه

به بین و بشنو شاد مان آنزمان / بوی شاد و نبود تراخود زیان

همین است ما را کنون یاد داد / گر با شد نگهدار پروردگار

A Rite to the Moon

FULL MOON, PHOTO BY P. NABARZ

In the lunar rite described here a simple approach is taken. That is drawing down the moon energy into a chalice/bowl while reciting ancient hymns to the moon and then drinking a clear liquid like water or mead or white wine, or elderflower wine, hence taking moon energy inside you that way (symbolically, metaphorically or literally depending on your views). It can be done as solo/couple or group. It is also not gender specific and it can be done outdoors on cold winter nights dressed in warm clothing.

There are three modus operandi here, a solo working, couple working and group working. In a solo working you are drawing the moon into yourself. In a two people scenario you can draw the moon into each other. In a group you want to draw the moon onto the whole group.

Here are some potential approaches that could be used in the rite:

If it is a solo working, a silver chalice could be used filled with water or mead or white wine or elderflower wine. Hold the chalice in a way that you can see the moon's reflection in it. When reciting the hymns focus on drawing down the moon energy into the chalice. The lunar hymns are recited in alternating fashion of looking at the moon and then looking at the reflection in the chalice. Once the hymn ends, drink from the chalice, visualising that you are drinking the lunar force and it is entering you.

In the couple scenario, both hold the chalice; hold the chalice in a way that you can both see the moon's reflection in it. Recite the hymns in turn; the lunar hymns are recited in alternating fashion of looking at the moon and then looking at the reflection in the chalice. While the hymns are being recited focus on drawing down the moon energy into the chalice. Once the hymn ends, drink some of the water in turns, visualising that you are drinking the lunar force and it is entering you.

In the group scenario each hymn is recited by a different member, again lunar hymns are recited in alternating fashion of looking at the moon and then looking at the reflection in the large silver bowl or chalice. Hold the chalice in a way that you can all see the moon's reflection in it. Depending on numbers it might be easier to place the bowl on the ground. When reciting the hymns focus on drawing down the moon energy into the bowl. Once the hymn ends, all participants drink from the bowl, visualising that you are drinking the lunar force and it is entering you.

There are several Greek, Roman, and Persian lunar hymns included here in the rite, it is worth noting despite the differences in the tradition of these lunar hymns all used here have several common themes. A major one of these is the connection of the moon to the Bull. In the Orphic Hymn we read:

*"Hear, Goddess queen, diffusing silver light,
Bull-horned and wandering thro' the gloom of Night."*[6]

And in the Zoroastrian hymn to the moon *Mah Niyayesh* we read:

"... glorification to the Moon that has the seed of the Bull. To the sole-created Bull. To the Bull of many species."[7]

And in PGM IV 2785-2890, prayer to Selene from the *Greek Magical Papyri* we read:

*"O Child of Morn who ride upon the Fierce Bulls,..
... Night-Crier, Bull-faced, loving Solitude,
Bull-headed, You have Eyes of Bulls..."*[8]

An excellent hymn that could also be used is in full is PGM IV 2785-2890, prayer to Selene from the *Greek Magical Papyri*.

Set up
- Location: a place with good visibility of the full moon
- Central fire lit (if needed due to cold) but kept to a size not to affect the night vision too much.
- Clothing: sensible outdoor clothing & footwear.
- Altar cloth to have stars on it.
- Silver bowl if a group working, silver chalice if solo working. Fill chalice or bowl with water, white wine or mead and place in circle.
- Offerings to moon, e.g. fruit, milk, etc.
- Food and drink to share.
- Incense

The standard opening mentioned in the chapter *'opening and closing of rites'* is used here.

Mystes 1 recites the *Orphic Hymn to the Stars*. This is then followed by:

Mystes 2:
(Facing the moon)
To the Moon. (The Hymns of Orpheus)
The fumigation from aromatics.
> "Hear, Goddess queen, diffusing silver light,
> Bull-horned and wandering thro' the gloom of Night.
> With stars surrounded, and with circuit wide
> Night's torch extending, thro' the heavens you ride:
> Female and Male with borrowed rays you shine,
> And now full-orbed, now tending to decline.
> Mother of ages, fruit-producing Moon,
> Whose amber orb makes Night's reflected noon:
> Lover of horses, splendid, queen of Night,
> All-seeing power bedecked with starry light.
> Lover of vigilance, the foe of strife,
> In peace rejoicing, and a prudent life:
> Fair lamp of Night, its ornament and friend,
> Who gives to Nature's works their destined end.
> Queen of the stars, all-wife Diana hail!
> Decked with a graceful robe and shining veil;
> Come, blessed Goddess, prudent, starry, bright,
> Come moony-lamp with chaste and splendid light,
> Shine on these sacred rites with prosperous rays,
> And please accept thy suppliant's mystic praise."[5]

Mystes 3:
(looks at the reflection of the moon in bowl or chalice)

Homeric Hymn XXXII. To Selene

"(ll. 1-13) And next, sweet voiced Muses, daughters of Zeus, well- skilled in song, tell of the long-winged Moon. From her immortal head a radiance is shown from heaven and embraces earth; and great is the beauty that ariseth from her shining light. The air, unlit before, glows with the light of her golden crown, and her rays beam clear, whensoever bright Selene having bathed her lovely body in the waters of Ocean, and donned her far-gleaming, shining team, drives on her long-maned horses at full speed, at eventime in the mid-month: then her great orbit is full and then her beams shine brightest as she increases. So she is a sure token and a sign to mortal men.

(ll. 14-16) Once the Son of Cronos was joined with her in love; and she conceived and bare a daughter Pandia, exceeding lovely amongst the deathless gods.

(ll. 17-20) Hail, white-armed goddess, bright Selene, mild, bright-tressed queen! And now I will leave you and sing the glories of men half-divine, whose deeds minstrels, the servants of the Muses, celebrate with lovely lips."[9]

Mystes 4:

(Facing the moon)

Mah Niyayesh (Moon Litany)

"0. In the name of God. May the majesty and glory of Ormazd, the beneficent lord, increase. (Hither) may come the purifier Moon, the Yazad Moon. Of all sins ... I repent.

1. Homage to Ahura Mazda. Homage to the Amesha Spentas. Homage to the Moon that has the seed of the Bull. Homage (to the Moon) when looked at. Homage with the look.

2. Propitiation to Ahura Mazda. ... I praise Asha (Truth). I proclaim ... of Ahurian Faith. Propitiation ... glorification to the Moon that has the seed of the Bull. To the sole-created Bull. To the Bull of many species. As (he is) the Lord that is to be chosen ... let one who knows it pronounce it to me.

3. Homage to Ahura Mazda .... Homage with the look.

4. How does the Moon wax? How does the Moon wane? Fifteen (days) does the Moon wax. Fifteen days does the moon wane. As long as (is) her waxing, so long the waning. So long (is) the waning, even as the waxing. Who (is it) through whom the Moon waxes (and) wanes, (other) than you?

5. We sacrifice to the Moon that has the seed of the Bull, the righteous and master of Asha (truth). Now I look at the Moon. Now I present myself to the Moon. Now I behold the brilliant Moon. I present myself to the brilliant Moon. There stand up the Amesha Spentas, they hold the glory. There stand the Amesha Spentas, they bestow the glory on the earth created by Ahura.

6. When the Moon warms with its light, then the golden-coloured plants always grow up together from the earth in the spring. (We sacrifice to) the new-moon days, the full-moon days, and the intervening seventh day. We sacrifice to the new-moon, the righteous, master of Asha. We sacrifice to the full-moon, the righteous, master of Asha. We sacrifice to the intervening day, the righteous, master of Asha.

7. I will sacrifice to the Moon that has the seed of the Bull, the bestower, radiant, glorious, possessed of water, possessed of warmth, possessed of knowledge, possessed of wealth, possessed of riches, possessed of discernment, possessed of weal, possessed of verdure, possessed of good, the bestower, the healing.

8. For his splendour and fortune I shall sacrifice to him with audible worship, the Moon that has the seed of the Bull, with libations. We sacrifice to the Moon that has the seed of the Bull, the righteous, master of Asha, With Haoma-containing milk ... and with correctly uttered words. We worship the male and female Entities in the worship of whom Ahura Mazda knows (there is (or: consists) what is) best (lit. better) according to Asha.

9. Y.A.V. I desire worship ... of the Moon that has the seed of the Bull, of the sole-created Bull, of cattle of all species. Ashem...

10. Give strength and victory. Give a satisfactory supply of cattle. Give a multitude of men, steadfast, belonging to the assembly, vanquishing, not vanquished, vanquishing adversaries at one stroke, vanquishing enemies at one stroke, of manifest help to the blessed.

11. O Yazads full of fortune! O Yazads full of healing! Manifest by your greatness, manifest be those of you who help when invoked. O waters give indeed just your own manifest fortune to the worshipper."[7]

Mystes 5:

(Looks at the reflection of the moon in the bowl or chalice)

7. Mah Yasht (Hymn to the Moon)

"0. May Ahura Mazda be rejoiced!....Ashem Vohu: Holiness is the best of all good....I confess myself a worshipper of Mazda, a follower of Zarathustra, one who hates the Daevas and obeys the laws of Ahura; For sacrifice, prayer, propitiation, and glorification unto [Havani], the holy and master of holiness....

Unto the Moon that keeps in it the seed of the Bull; unto the only-created Bull and unto the Bull of many species;

Be propitiation, with sacrifice, prayer, propitiation, and glorification.

Yatha ahu vairyo: The will of the Lord is the law of holiness....

1. Hail to Ahura Mazda! Hail to the Amesha-Spentas! Hail to the Moon that keeps in it the seed of the Bull! Hail to thee when we look at thee! Hail to thee when thou lookest at us!

2. How does the moon wax? How does the moon wane?

For fifteen days does the moon wax; for fifteen days does the moon wane. As long as her waxing, so long is the waning; as long as her waning, so long is the waxing.

Who is there but thee who makes the moon wax and wane?
3. We sacrifice unto the Moon that keeps in it the seed of the Bull, the holy and master of holiness.
Here I look at the moon, here I perceive the moon; here I look at the light of the moon, here I perceive the light of the moon. The Amesha-Spentas stand up holding its glory; the Amesha-Spentas stand up, pouring its glory upon the earth, made by Mazda.
4. And when the light of the moon waxes warmer, golden-hued plants grow on from the earth during the spring.
We sacrifice unto the new moons, the full moons, and the Vishaptathas.
We sacrifice unto the new moon, the holy and master of holiness;
We sacrifice unto the full moon, the holy and master of holiness;
We sacrifice unto the Vishaptatha, the holy and master of holiness.
5. I will sacrifice unto the Moon, that keeps in it the seed of the Bull, the liberal, bright, glorious, water-giving, warmth-giving, wisdom-giving, wealth-giving, riches-giving, thoughtfulness-giving, weal-giving, freshness-giving, prosperity-giving, the liberal, the healing.
6. For its brightness and glory, I will offer unto it a sacrifice worth being heard, namely, unto the Moon that keeps in it the seed of the Bull.
Unto the Moon that keeps in it the seed of the Bull, we offer up the libations, the Haoma and meat, the baresma, the wisdom of the tongue, the holy spells, the speech, the deeds, the libations, and the rightly-spoken words. Yenghe hatam: All those beings of whom Ahura Mazda....
7. Yatha ahu vairyo: The will of the Lord is the law of holiness....
I bless the sacrifice and prayer, and the strength and vigour of the Moon, that keeps in it the seed of the Bull, and of the only-created Bull, and of the Bull of many species.
Ashem Vohu: Holiness is the best of all good.
Give unto that man brightness and glory, give him health of body... give him the bright, all-happy, blissful abode of the holy Ones." [7]

- ⊕ Once the hymn ends, drink some of the water from the bowl, visualising that you are drinking the lunar force and it is entering you.
- ⊕ Sit, face the moon, and mediate on all that has been recited and energy you have taken into yourself.
- ⊕ You might be inspired and moved to give voice to the lunar current you have invoked.
- ⊕ Pour your biodegradable offering e.g. fruit, milk.
- ⊕ Final thanks to the Moon.

The standard closing mentioned in the chapter *'opening and closing of rites'* is used here. Mystes 1 recites the closing Orphic hymn to the stars. This is followed by having something to eat and drink. Clear the space.

References:
1. *Drawing Down the Moon,* The Gardnerian Book of Shadows, by Gerald Gardner.
2. *The Charge of the Goddess,* The Gardnerian Book of Shadows, by Gerald Gardner.
3. *Liber XV* The Gnostic Mass by Aleister Crowley.
4. *Liber AL vel Legis* by Aleister Crowley.
5. *The Pari-Persian Burj-Namah,* or Book of Omens from the Moon. Louis H. Gray; 1910; in *Journal of the American Oriental Society*, Vol. 30.4:336-42.
6. *The Hymns of Orpheus* translated by Thomas Taylor 1792.
7. *Avesta: Khorda Avesta* (Book of Common Prayer) Translation by James Darmesteter (From Sacred Books of the East, American Edition, 1898.)
8. Opening lines from PGM IV 2785-2890, prayer to Selene from *The Greek Magical Papyri in Translation: Including the Demotic Spells* by Hans Dieter Betz. University Of Chicago Press; 2nd edition, 1997, pp90-92.
9. *The Homeric Hymns* translated by Hugh G. Evelyn-White, 1914.

Further reading:
If interested in the relationship between moon and the Zodiac signs see:
Chapter 5 Manzail–al–Qamar the 28 Mansions of the Moon in *Celestial Magic: Principles and Practises of the Talismanic Art* by Nigel Jackson, Capall Bann Publishing, 2003.
Mansions of the Moon Using the Lunar Mansions for Magic & Astrology by Christopher Warnock.
http://www.renaissanceastrology.com/mansionsmoonbook.html
The lunar clock section in Chapter 5 'Twenty eight' in *Tankhem: Meditations on Seth Magick* by Mogg Morgan, Mandrake of Oxford, 2003 and chapters Oracles & Lunar Omina / Lunar diary in *Supernatural Assault in Ancient Egypt: Seth, Renpet and Moon Magick* by Mogg Morgan, Mandrake of Oxford, 2008.
Praise to the Moon: Magic and Myth of the Lunar Cycle by Elen Hawke, Llewellyn Publications, 2002.

Notes:

SEVEN PLANETS

INTRODUCTION

This stellar ceremony which relates to the Neo-Platonic based cosmology involves a number of deities: Pales (mother earth), Mercury, Venus, Mars, Jupiter, Moon, Sun, and Saturn. This is a rite of a magical ascent from Earth through the seven gates, which are each of the aforementioned planetary spheres and deities. The seven planets (the wandering stars) have symbolic connections to metals according to the theology of Mithraism, as it was provided by Celsus, the Roman writer of the second century AD:

> *"After this, Celsus, desiring to exhibit his learning in his treatise against us, quotes also certain Persian mysteries, where he says: "These things are obscurely hinted at in the accounts of the Persians, and especially in the mysteries of Mithras, which are celebrated amongst them. For in the latter there is a representation of the two heavenly revolutions,-of the movement, viz., of the fixed stars, and of that which take place among the planets, and of the passage of the soul through these. The representation is of the following nature: There is a ladder with lofty gates and on the top of it an eighth gate. The first gate consists of lead, the second of tin, the third of copper, the fourth of iron, the fifth of a mixture of metals, the sixth of silver, and the seventh of gold. The first gate they assign to Saturn, indicating by the lead the slowness of this star; the second to Venus, comparing her to the splendour and softness of tin; the third to Jupiter, being firm and solid; the fourth to Mercury, for both Mercury and iron are fit to endure all things, and are money-making and laborious; the fifth to Mars, because, being composed of a mixture of metals, it is varied and unequal; the sixth, of silver, to the Moon; the seventh, of gold, to the Sun,-thus imitating the different colours of the two latter." He next proceeds to examine the reason of the stars being arranged in this order, which is symbolized by the names of the rest of matter. Musical reasons, moreover, are added or quoted by the Persian theology; and to these, again, he strives to add a second explanation, connected also with musical considerations."*
>
> - Origen. Against Celsus[1]

The principle of ascension is the reversal of the process of birth on Earth; the souls entered via the constellation of Cancer, the point of genesis and left via the constellation of Capricorn the point of apogenesis. A view that is seen as:

> *"The soul, having started on its downward course from the intersection of the zodiac and the Milk Way to the successive spheres lying beneath, as it passes through these spheres, not only takes on the afore-mentioned envelopment in each sphere by approaching a luminous body, but also acquires each of the attributes which it will exercise later. In the sphere of Saturn it obtains reason and understanding, in Jupiter sphere the power to act, in Mars' sphere a bold spirit, in the Sun's sphere sense-perception and imagination. In Venus' sphere the impulse of passion, in Mercury's sphere the ability to speak and interpret and in the lunar sphere the function of the moulding and increasing bodies."*
> *- From Platonist Macrobius commentary on Cicero's 'Scipio's dream' fifth century A.D.*[2]

One of the recommended further readings for Planetary rites is the book *Practical Planetary Magick* by Sorita d'Este & David Rankine (Avalonia, 2007).

A point to bear in mind, is that the planets in some views are not beneficent, unlike the stars. In Zoroastrianism the while the stars are created by Ahura Mazda the Planets are created by Ahriman in opposition to the stars. This is in line with some aspects of Mandean Planetary talismanic magic where the talismans are not made to channel the planet but to hold its influence at bay!

The rite of the seven planets below is to guide the magician through the gates of the planet and to the stars. The goal is to reach beyond the seven planetary spheres and reach the realm of the stars.

Rite of the Seven Planets

This rite can be performed as a group ceremony for eight people; one candidate and seven planetary initiators, the candidate or journey person walks up the hill to each planet where s/he hears the invocation to the planet. This rite can also be performed as a solo working, where the individual performs all the invocations.

- ⊕ A bonfire (if outdoors) will be lit to mark the occasion at sunset.
- ⊕ Give plenty of time for clearing and setting up the ritual space.
- ⊕ The seven planetary representatives should wear clothes or robes in colours or symbols relating to the planet, for example *the Picatrix (Ghayat al Hikam)* based schema could be adapted. This is black robe or clothes for Saturn, yellow or white for Jupiter, red for Mars, gold for Sun, white or green for Venus, silver or white for Moon, light blue for Mercury.[3]

The order followed for the invocation of seven planetary deities is: Mercury, Venus, Mars, Jupiter, Moon, Sun, Saturn. Each person *'becomes'* the planet they calling on. Each planet is invoked using the Mystical Hymns of Orpheus.[4]

Props:

- ⊕ Place seven lit torches or large candles creating a path that leads to the bonfire.
- ⊕ Set up an altar with a pictures or statues of all seven deities: Mercury, Venus, Mars, Jupiter, Moon, Sun, and Saturn.
- ⊕ The symbols of seven planetary deities should be present, for example:
  - o A feather, a caduceus, for Mercury.
  - o A lamp, veil, spring water in cup for Venus.
  - o Dagger, spear, shield for Mars.
  - o Sistrum, incense, fire tongs & incense burner for Jupiter.
  - o Honey & Scythe for Moon.
  - o A large flaming torch, or a (large candle in sun candle holder), a crown for Sun.
  - o Staff, a dagger, and a libation bowl for Saturn.
  - o Corn/wheat.

- The planetary incenses to be burned for the Orphic hymns
- Food and drinks for the feast.
- If performed indoor and music could be played: a relevant CD is *Secrets of the Heavens* which are seven planetary invocations performed by Catherine King, Mark Tucker, and Mark Rylance in the spirit of Orphic singing, written by the 15th century philosopher Marsilio Ficino.

The standard opening mentioned in the chapter *'opening and closing of rites'* is used here. This is then followed by hailing the planet is the seven directions, that is above, below and within in addition to the four cardinal positions.

All: *Fertile Earth Pales who procreates everything.*

Seven directions are greeted by each person in their own words:
- Mercury opens East (Air),
- Venus opens West (water)
- Mars opens North (Earth)
- Jupiter opens South (Fire)
- Moon opens below (underworld)
- Sun opens above (upper world/ starry sky)
- Saturn opens within (boundary of Space).

Followed by **Mercury** saying:
"O Primal Origin of my origination; Thou Primal Substance of my substance; First Breath of breath, the breath that is in me; First Fire, God-given for the Blending of the blendings in me, [First Fire] of fire in me; First Water of [my] water. The water in me; Primal Earth essence of the earthy essence in me; Thou Perfect Body of me – N.N. [your name], son of N.N. (fem.)[your mother's name] – fashioned by Honoured Arm and Incorruptible Right Hand, in World that's lightless, yet radiant with Light, [in World] that's soulless, yet filled full of Soul!"[5]

Venus:
"The soul, having started on its downward course from the intersection of the zodiac and the Milky Way to the successive spheres lying beneath, as it passes through these spheres, not only takes on the afore-mentioned envelopment in each sphere by approaching a luminous body, but also acquires each of the attributes which it will exercise later. In the sphere of Saturn it

obtains reason and understanding, in Jupiter sphere the power to act, in Mars' sphere a bold spirit, in the Sun's sphere sense-perception and imagination. In Venus' sphere the impulse of passion, in Mercury's sphere the ability to speak and interpret and in the lunar sphere the function of the moulding and increasing bodies."[2]

Invocation of seven planetary deities: Mercury, Venus, Mars, Jupiter, Moon, Sun, Saturn. Each person *'becomes'* the planet they calling on. Each planet is invoked using the *Mystical Hymns of Orpheus.*[4]

☿

The Orphic Hymn to Mercury XXVII.
(The Fumigation from Frankincense).
"
*"Hermes, draw near, and to my prayer incline,
Angel of Jove, and Maia's son divine;
Studious of contests, ruler of mankind,
With heart almighty, and a prudent mind.
Celestial messenger, of various skill,
Whose powerful arts could watchful Argus kill:
With winged feet, 'tis thine thro' air to course,
O friend of man, and prophet of discourse:
Great life-supporter, to rejoice is thine,
In arts gymnastic, and in fraud divine:
With power endued all language to explain,
Of care the loos'ner, and the source of gain.
Whose hand contains of blameless peace the rod,
Corucian, blessed, profitable God;
Of various speech, whose aid in works we find,
And in necessities to mortals kind:
Dire weapon of the tongue, which men revere,
Be present, Hermes, and thy suppliant hear;
Assist my works, conclude my life with peace,
Give graceful speech, and me memory's increase."*[4]

♀

The Orphic Hymn to Venus

*"Heavenly, illustrious, laughter-loving queen,
Sea-born, night-loving, of an awful mien;
Crafty, from whom necessity first came,*

Producing, nightly, all-connecting dame:
'This thine the world with harmony to join,
For all things spring from thee, O power divine.
The triple Fates are ruled by thy decree,
And all productions yield alike to thee:
Whatever the heavens, encircling all contain,
Earth fruit-producing, and the stormy main,
Thy sway confesses, and obeys thy nod,
Awful attendant of the brumal God:
Goddess of marriage, charming to the sight,
Mother of Loves, whom banqueting delight;
Source of persuasion, secret, favouring queen,
Illustrious born, apparent and unseen:
Spousal, lupercal, and to men inclined,
Prolific, most-desired, life-giving., kind:
Great sceptre-bearer of the Gods, 'tis thine,
Mortals in necessary bands to join;
And every tribe of savage monsters dire
In magic chains to bind, thro' mad desire.
Come, Cyprus-born, and to my prayer incline,
Whether exalted in the heavens you shine,
Or pleased in Syria's temple to preside,
Or o'er the' Egyptian plains thy car to guide,
Fashioned of gold; and near its sacred flood,
Fertile and famed to fix thy blest abode;
Or if rejoicing in the azure shores,
Near where the sea with foaming billows roars,
The circling choirs of mortals, thy delight,
Or beauteous nymphs, with eyes cerulean bright,
Pleased by the dusty banks renowned of old,
To drive thy rapid, two-yoked car of gold;
Or if in Cyprus with thy mother fair,
Where married females praise thee every year,
And beauteous virgins in the chorus join,
Adonis pure to sing and thee divine;
Come, all-attractive to my prayer inclined,
For thee, I call, with holy, reverent mind."[4]

♂

The Orphic Hymn to Mars
(The Fumigation from Frankincense)

"Magnanimous, unconquered, boisterous Mars,
In darts rejoicing, and in bloody wars
Fierce and untamed, whose mighty power can make
The strongest walls from their foundations shake:
Mortal destroying king, defiled with gore,

Pleased with war's dreadful and tumultuous roar:
Thee, human blood, and swords, and spears delight,
And the dire ruin of mad savage fight.
Stay, furious contests, and avenging strife,
Whose works with woe, embitter human life;
To lovely Venus, and to Bacchus yield,
To Ceres give the weapons of the field;
Encourage peace, to gentle works inclined,
And give abundance, with benignant mind."* [4]

♃

The Orphic Hymn to Jupiter
(The Fumigation from Storax)

"O Jove much-honoured, Jove supremely great,
To thee our holy rites we consecrate,
Our prayers and expiations, king divine,
For all things round thy head exalted shine.
The earth is thine, and mountains swelling high,
The sea profound, and all within the sky.
Saturnian king, descending from above,
Magnanimous, commanding, sceptred Jove;
All-parent, principle and end of all,
Whose power almighty, shakes this earthly ball;
Even Nature trembles at thy mighty nod,
Loud-sounding, armed with lightning, thundering God.
Source of abundance, purifying king,
O various-formed from whom all natures spring;
Propitious hear my prayer, give blameless health,
With peace divine, and necessary wealth. "[4]

☾

The Orphic Hymn to the Moon
(The Fumigation from Aromatics)

"Hear, Goddess queen, diffusing silver light,
Bull-horned and wandering thro' the gloom of Night.
With stars surrounded, and with circuit wide
Night's torch extending, thro' the heavens you ride:
Female and Male with borrowed rays you shine,
And now full-orbed, now tending to decline.
Mother of ages, fruit-producing Moon,
Whose amber orb makes Night's reflected noon:
Lover of horses, splendid, queen of Night,
All-seeing power bedecked with starry light.

Lover of vigilance, the foe of strife,
In peace rejoicing, and a prudent life:
Fair lamp of Night, its ornament and friend,
Who giv'st to Nature's works their destined end.
Queen of the stars, all-wife Diana hail!
Decked with a graceful robe and shining veil;
Come, blessed Goddess, prudent, starry, bright,
Come moony-lamp with chaste and splendid light,
Shine on these sacred rites with prosperous rays,
And pleased accept thy suppliant's mystic praise."[4]

The Orphic Hymn to the Sun
(The Fumigation from Frankincense and Manna)

"Hear golden Titan, whose eternal eye
With broad survey, illumines all the sky.
Self-born, unwearied in diffusing light,
And to all eyes the mirror of delight:
Lord of the seasons, with thy fiery car
And leaping coursers, beaming light from far:
With thy right hand the source of morning light,
And with thy left the father of the night.
Agile and vigorous, venerable Sun,
Fiery and bright around the heavens you run.
Foe to the wicked, but the good man's guide,
O'er all his steps propitious you preside:
With various founding, golden lyre, 'tis mine
To fill the world with harmony divine.
Father of ages, guide of prosperous deeds,
The world's commander, borne by lucid steeds,
Immortal Jove, all-searching, bearing light,
Source of existence, pure and fiery bright
Bearer of fruit, almighty lord of years,
Agile and warm, whom every power reveres.
Great eye of Nature and the starry skies,
Doomed with immortal flames to set and rise
Dispensing justice, lover of the stream,
The world's great despot, and o'er all supreme.
Faithful defender, and the eye of right,
Of steeds the ruler, and of life the light:
With founding whip four fiery steeds you guide,
When in the car of day you glorious ride.
Propitious on these mystic labours shine,
And bless thy suppliants with a life divine."[4]

The Orphic Hymn to Saturn
(The Fumigation from Storax)

"Ethereal father, mighty Titan, hear,
Great fire of Gods and men, whom all revere:
Endued with various council, pure and strong,
To whom perfection and decrease belong.
Consumed by thee all forms that hourly die,
By thee restored, their former place supply;
The world immense in everlasting chains,
Strong and ineffable thy power contains
Father of vast eternity, divine,
O mighty Saturn, various speech is thine: Blossom of earth and
of the starry skies,
Husband of Rhea, and Prometheus wife.
Obstetric Nature, venerable root,
From which the various forms of being shoot;
No parts peculiar can thy power enclose,
Diffused thro' all, from which the world arose,
O, best of beings, of a subtle mind,
Propitious hear to holy prayers inclined;
The sacred rites benevolent attend,
And grant a blameless life, a blessed end."[4]

- ⊕ Sit and mediate on all that has been recited and energy you have taken into yourself.
- ⊕ You might be inspired and moved to give voice to the planetary current you have invoked.
- ⊕ Leave your biodegradable offering.
- ⊕ Saying of thanks to the spirits of the place.

The standard closing mentioned in the chapter *'opening and closing of rites'* is used here. This is followed by having something to eat and drink. Then clear the space.

References

Origen. *Against Celsus* http://www.ccel.org/fathers2/ANF-04/anf04-61.htm#P10231_2711351

From Platonist Macrobius commentary on Cicero's *Scipio's dream* fifth century AD.

Manfred Clauss *The Roman cult of Mithras* p11.

The Picatrix or Ghayat al Hikam: The Premier Grimoire of Astrological Magic, Book III, Chapter 3 translated by Christopher Warnock, Esq.

http://www.renaissanceastrology.com/picatrixplanetclothes.html

and *The Picatrix* book III, Chapter 3. Figures, dyes, clothing, incenses of the planets and also dyes of the decans of the signs. Mike Rock.

http://picatrix.mike-rock.com/book3/p3ch3.php

The Hymns of Orpheus translated by Thomas Taylor 1792. http://www.sacred-texts.com/cla/hoo/index.htm and also on http://www.renaissanceastrology.com

Mithras Liturgy adapted here from that of G.R.S. Mead, from *A Mithraic Ritual*, 1907.

Further reading:

Picatrix Ghayat al Hakim or The Goal of the Wise, Atallah, Hashem (Trans); Kiesel, William (Ed), Ouroboros Press, 2002.

The Picatrix or Ghayat al Hikam: The Premier Grimoire of Astrological Magic, Christopher Warnock, Esq. A very comprehensive site with translations, guide books and videos.

http://www.renaissanceastrology.com/picatrix.html

The Picatrix site by Mike Rock http://picatrix.mike-rock.com

Practical Planetary Magick by Sorita d'Este & David Rankine, Avalonia, 2007.

The Magus: Or Celestial Intelligencer by Francis Barrett, Nonsuch publishing Ltd. 2007.

Notes:

Cygnus

Northern Cross

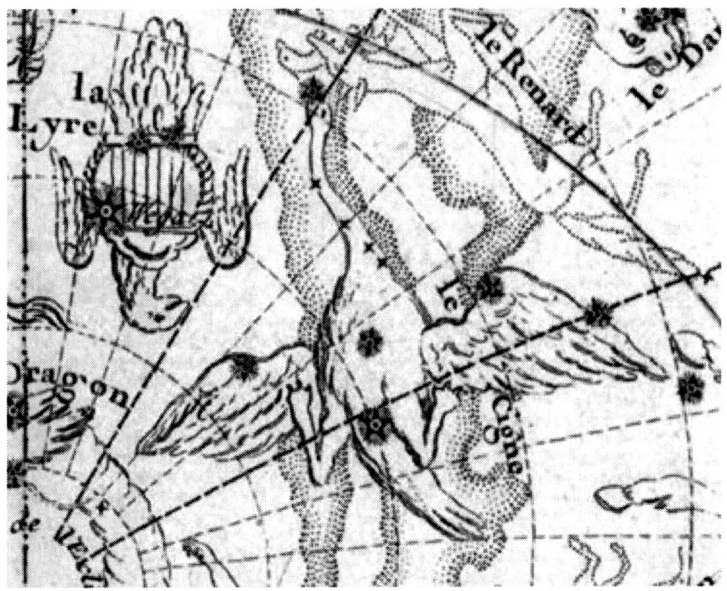

ATLAS CÉLESTE DE FLAMSTÉED

Introduction

"Now there stands far from the haunts of men the Mount Alborz, whose head touched the stars, and never had mortal foot been planted upon its crest. And upon it had the Simurgh, the bird of marvel, build her nest. Of ebony and of sandal-wood did she build it, and twined it with aloes, so that it was like unto a king's house, and the evil sway of Saturn could not reach thereto."

- Shah Nameh by Ferdowsi.[1]

The legend of Cygnus is a tale of camaraderie and brotherly love. In Greek Mythology, the great bird constellation was called Cygnus. According to one legend: Cycnus, the King of Liguria, was friends with Phaethon, the son of Helios (Apollo). Phaethon drove the sun's chariot for a day, which was a disaster, as he could not control the fiery horses of the sun's chariot and nearly set the whole world on fire. Ovid's tale of Phaeton in *Metamorphoses* is a recommended read, as it contains emotive descriptions of the Zodiac and the heavens. Phaethon's drive was brought to an end when he saw the constellation Scorpio, and Jupiter struck him with a lightning bolt. Phaeton fell from the heavens to the earth burning like a meteorite, and plunged into the river Eridanus. Aratus in the *Phaenomena* describes the river Eridanus as the river of many tears, referring to those shed by Phaethon's sisters, the Heliades. The river Eridanus is the modern day river Po in Italy. Michelangelo Buonarotti's drawing of the fall of Phaeton is a very powerful image, and it is recommended that you have a copy of it for your reference during your study of the Cygnus chapter.

Cygnus was heartbroken from the death of Phaethon, and left his kingdom to wander the land and bury Phaethon's remains; for his devotion, Jupiter transformed him into a swan (Cygnus).[2]

PHOTO BY P. NABARZ

The star Deneb in the Cygnus constellation is part of the summer triangle, the other two points of the triangle are the star Vega in Lyra and the star Altair in Aquila (Eagle). The triangle can act as marker for identifying neighbouring constellations in the night sky. The Swan acting as Eagle's wingman as they fly in the night sky! Aratus in *Phaenomena* refers to the Eagle as the *'Storm Bird'*, when the night is waning and it rises, storms occur. The Eagle is the messenger of Zeus and it is partnered with Lyra or the Vulture constellation. Lyra is shown as Orpheus' harp, and sometimes a

Vulture carries the harp. The winter triangle essentially connects the three birds around the Milky Way together.

Another story behind the naming of the swan constellation can be seen as;

> "... The swan might well be the image of the divinely inspired poet, of the sacred priesthood, of the white-robed druid, of the Norse Skald and so on. At first sight the myth of Leda would seem to bear the same interpretation of the symbol of the swan as male and diurnal. However, closer examination reveals that if Zeus changed himself into a swan to come to Leda, this was, as the Greek myth explains, only after she 'had turned herself into a goose to escape him'. Now, as we have seen, the goose is an avatar of the swan in its female and lunar acceptation, so that the loves of swan- Zeus and goose-Leda stand for the bipolarization of the symbol. This leads one to presume that the Greeks intentionally brought together these two meanings, the diurnal and the nocturnal, to make the swan a hermaphrodite symbol in which Leda and her divine lover are really only one..."[3]

The swan is also a part of alchemical symbolism, a marriage of opposites like fire and water a sign of hermaphroditism, and this perhaps is the mystery W.B. Yeats is trying to explain in his poem *'Leda and the Swan'* and the poem *'His Phoenix'*. Swans play an important role in Yeats' poems, and reappear in works such as *'The Wild Swans at the Coole'* and *'Baile and Aillinn'*.[4]

PHOTO BY P. NABARZ

Back in December 2001 I was involved with starting an experimental Druid Esoteric group. As part of creating the space, I carried out a meditation on this theme at the full moon with the specific site in Oxfordshire in mind as the *'physical'* site of the Grove; this site being in close proximity to the river. In the place where we held the bonfire, I saw a great fire in shape of a phoenix, the fire bird of continuous rebirth and death, the one that rises from the ashes. The phoenix was golden/red and kept changing colour, and was looking through the trees toward the river. I then looked at the river Thames (Isis) that flowed by, and saw a beautiful majestic Swan. The Swan and the Phoenix were staring at each other lovingly, and they began some sort of bird-dance, at which point due to the intensity of it, I came out of the meditation.

There were several ways of interpreting this, one was that the site which was a Victorian rubbish dump had now turned into woodland again, and the group was part of the *'reclaiming'* of the land; as a Neo-Druid group putting energy into the site by acts like these and holding rites there. This is the phoenix rising from the ashes, and in the last 80 years, trees and plants are returning to a place where once it was desolate. The Swan is the sacred river, and is connected to Oxford, a bird which is sometimes shown with St. Friedswide, the patron Saint of Oxford, or the goddess that protects the Ox-ford. For many, Friedswide is also connected to the goddess Brigid, perhaps as an Anglo-Christian version. Brigid is also represented by swans; perhaps the Swan is the Goddess who is always there and doesn't die; the constant river flow/river of life, while the phoenix is the god that keeps dying and being born again?

Interestingly, the first recorded attempt at a Druid revival took place in Oxford. According to Dr. Michel Raoult in the book *Druid Renaissance*:

> *"It is said that a grove of Druids known as Cor Emrys established in the city of Oxford in 1066 CE, this name means 'City of Ambrosia' and is rich in innuendo and invokes at the same time the Pleiades constellation, the earth's magnetism, the circle of the giants of Ambrius Hill - the megalithic, astronomic calendar of Stonehenge - the traditions of Atlantis and Hyperborea, and characters such as those in the Round Table cycle of Breton novels."*[5]

No one knows how long the 1066 grove operated, but there was a second Druid Grove formed in 1245 in Oxford known as the Mount-Haemus Grove. Again, it is uncertain how long this second revival lasted, but there was a third revival at some point, as there were representatives of *'an Oxford Grove'* present in the well known meeting in the Apple Tree Tavern on 22nd September 1717, where modern Druidry was born. The link between Oxford and Druidry is an interesting one, as Oxford's Albion Lodge Druid group was the group Winston Churchill was initiated into in 1908.

To bring us back to the Swan and the Phoenix, during another meditation I became aware of a link between the two. The connecting point appeared to be the Cygnus (Swan) constellation; what appeared to be two separate currents and metaphors meet in Cygnus. The watery majestic Swan and the fiery ever changing Phoenix shared a common symbol, the Cygnus constellation. From the Persian Phoenix the Simurgh or the Arabic Roc and Greek we see a thread that links the constellation Cygnus to both water and fire birds. The Swan and Phoenix grove ceased operation in 2004, however I was part of a triad of Druids, which in 2007 founded another Druid Grove in Oxford that was called: *'Nemeton of the Stars'*. The working with constellations that began with the Cygnus constellation slowly built up with rites to different constellations over the next few years, and reached its apex in form of writing this book on *'Stellar Magic'* and working with *'Nemeton of the Stars'* and becoming a Hierophant.

I also feel it is important to expand on the spiritual aspect of Oxford and its connection, or rather, the magical side of Oxford. The magical well in Oxford is one that many writers have drawn from, Lewis Carroll, C. S. Lewis, J. R. R. Tolkien and Phillip Pullman to name a few. According to the Welsh epic *The Mabinogion*, Oxford is at the centre of England, as this is where the two dragons meet (see the later Draco constellation chapter for more details) and the place acts as an Omphalos. For this I have written the following to celebrate this magical well.

PHOTO BY P. NABARZ

ASTRAL TOUR OF OXON (PART I- III)

Part I Moonlight
(Written at full moon 7 December 2003.)

"Once a man had a dream of people walking together in equality,
a place where you can 'do what thou wilt'
to grow in mind, body, and spirit,
without fear of persecution or prejudice.

A place where the mosque, church, synagogue, temple,
off licenses, strip joints, dope dealers are all next door to each other.
This is Crowley (Cowley) Rd, where there is no restriction,
follow your own Will, and see the dream of equality as reality.

Head to CS Lewis's Headington neighbourhood,
walk on Shotover Hill and look for its hidden carved Giant.
I wonder if Lewis was alive today would he
approve of the 'Headington Swingers Club?'

Maybe you'd prefer the Ents in Merton College grounds,
or the door to Moria painted on dining hall door.
Say "Mellon" and enter, and share a drink
with J.R.R. Tolkien's ghost in The Bird and Baby.

If a fog comes down when you are in Christ Church,
Merton, or New College, you will know the meaning
of time travel. Is it 1900? 1800? 1700? The fog rolls in
the college corridors and pushes away time.
The music from HolyWell music room will lead you
back to the present.

Beware of the Bodleian library, always there,
she entices your mind with her
thousand years of preserved knowledge,
and with her dark caverns under Broad Street,
she beckons you to her web.

Isis will catch your eye, with her moist blue skin
and deep black eyes, her slender body stretches
along the Thames. Boats and Punts glide over her
like hairbrush through her beautiful hair.
At midday she shines golden and bright,
At midnight she shines silver and mysterious,
Beckoning you in for a skinny dipping,
Enflaming your love, feeding your passion.
The Kassam stadium is up for sale

*for a one pound! May be one day Oxford United
will go up the football league table,
but then that may be that's one dream too far!*

*If you go down the woods at night,
you are sure of a big surprise, witches and magicians,
dancing around bonfires, chanting and drumming.
Witches don't fly on broomsticks, but they certainly
carry big staffs and long swords.
By witches, I don't mean the Hogwarts bunch
in Christ Church. I mean descendants
of WB Yeats and Dr. John Dee.*

*If world treasure is the aim of your quest,
look no further than the Ashmolean or Pitt Rivers,
a complete Egyptian Temple, Aboriginal religious artefacts,
Roman Mithraic statues, Greek vases, and of course
the shrunken heads.*

*From there, blood red Keble College
is a stone's throw away, with
its Holman-Hunt's 'The Light of the World',
remember the door to thy self and enlightenment opens inwards.*

*If you are in the right headspace you might see
the Mabinogion's two dragons that sleep under Oxford,
one of their tails being Magdalen College tower,
the other tail being St. Michael's tower.
Their scales and ridges stick up through ground
all over the city, giving rise to the Oxford 'Spires'.*

*St. Friedswide, Patron Saint of Oxford fortunately
strokes the heads of the dragons and keeps them calm,
otherwise the Uffington White horse might bolt
along Ridgeway, and no Smith could shoe her then.*

*If you head out of Oxen towards the North,
you might RollRight back into Oxford again,
best to follow the river South and pay the ferryman at
Duchess Dykes and Whittenham Clumps.*

*Go for a walk along the Science Park,
and recall Fleming's miracle work,
or go straight to the Lamb and Flag
for a pint of Old Peculiar.*

*It's not all joyous, there is a dark side too,
Campsfield prison for strangers in strange land,*

or the B52 bombers flying off from Brize Norton,
to drop death 1000 miles away.

I wonder does God still visit Frevds Church
on Sundays since it turned into a bar?
Or does he prefer watching a French film in
Phoenix cinema in Jericho? I am sure I saw a book
by him in the Inner Bookshop,
'Sacred Landscape, God is Everything'.

With that thought, I let myself gently
be engulfed by the wings of the Isis River
and visions of the Ox,
and dream of 'City of Ambrosia'.

If you think it's all heads in clouds here,
remember this is the home of BMW,
and this little tale
has just been a Mini adventure."

Part II Age
(Written January 2004)

"Perhaps you'll find yourself walking up
Sunderland Avenue, beware of Philip Pullman's
doorway leading to parallel Oxford- Cittagazze.
There is plenty to see here without side stepping,
just follow the Lewis Carrol's white rabbit and go
down Binsey Holy Well. Alice will be your guide
to the Fly Agaric mushroom.

Look through the 1000 year old Yew tree
in Iffley Church and see the old Christian
Pilgrim's route from Abingdon Abbey,
to St. Bartholomew's Holy Well on Cowley Rd.
A visit to St. Bart's Well is said to lead
to a decrease of 400 years from your purgatory!

I asked the old Woman by Northgate
and St Michel's Saxon Tower.
how old is she?
She didn't reply in words, but showed me her way

Then I saw before the City,
the Round huts on Port Meadow,
and there was a strong black
Ox grazing in the fields;

before that a beautiful White Horse

running in the Valley,
followed by numerous other beasts;

before that the old Ridgeway twisting
like a serpent, on it the old Smith,
the old Linddington and Barbury Castle Hills
leading to Avebury in the South
and Ivinghoe Beacon in the North.

Before that, the river, the Thame-Isis , flowing.
Before that a very old, yet fully blossoming tree.
(I guess that is where Tolkien's inspiration
for the White Tree of Gondor came from!)

Before that, I saw the old Woman again,
she appears no older than now,
all this time has been
a brief moment for her."

Part III Deeg Jush (Seething Cauldron)
(Written 20 June 2004)

"At Summer Solstice, the longest day,
The symbolic height of power of light (Nur).
Under the eye of Mithra (Mehr-kindness): the Sun,
In the Old Windmill, the Pir is turning the Millstone,
metamorphosing the soul-grain of the Sufis into
bread and cakes of light to nourish all mankind.

We little raindrops, rush forth,
like the Irish Bard Taliesin,
into the Deeg Jush -
the cauldron of transformation
to be boiled and changed.

In the 'Jam Khaneh' –the Gathering House,
All have gathered, seen and unseen,
from Earth to the Seven Heavens.
All religions and their gods across
time and space stand
shoulder to shoulder in the 'Jam Khaneh'.
A Shiva statute next to a Golden Buddha,
Christ next to Allah,
next to the Horned Deer
of our cave dwelling ancestors.

People too have gathered from all corners
of this blue tear in space we call home.
Young and old, man and woman,

*from different races and cultures and
continents: Asia, Africa, Europe,
the Americas, Australia,
all have gathered in
the `Jam Khaneh'.*

*Words of the Pir echoes: "5000 year old Aryan
(Indo-European) creed of Divine Unity,
Love and Chivalry spread across
the Old World by the Aryan people".
The outer label might have altered
through the millennia, Dervish, Sufi, Magi,
Duir, Druids, Brahmins, ... but its heart
has changed little in those
in the 'Land of the Aryans':
Eire (Ireland) to Iran.
The lit torch is kept alive by many now,
and has gone beyond the land of
Aryans, bringing light into many dark places.*

*In the 'Jam Khaneh', we,
like little points of light,
form a galaxy, all circling the
Qutub (pole) during Zeker –
the remembrance.
Outside of this Temple of Love,
saplings planted by us in rich soil of Oxon
many moons ago, are now tall groves
towering above our heads.*

*In the Oak groves, the doorway tree
of Duir opens a gateway to Otherworld.
Silver Birch tree, shimmering Lady of the Woods,
dances and moves her slender white arms
to the sound of the Tonbak -drum.
The smell of roses is intoxicating all,
in this Golestan of Love.
In the fruitful Apple Orchards,
the meaning of Avalon: Isle of Apples (Britain)
becomes clear.*

*The trees, the flowers, even the farmer's cows
and the bees are joining the song and dance of Unity.
Hu, Hu, Hu.
All is One and One is All.
Remember: Unity, Love, Chivalry
Haq, Haq, Haq.
'Everything' is turning, whirling
around the Qutub during ecstasy of Sama.
An eternity caught in a moment.*

Hu, Hu, Hu.

*The constellation Cygnus flying
in the Milky Way, it is very much
a swan swimming in the river Isis.
As above, as below."*

More recently there has been a detailed study of Cygnus constellation by Andrew Collins in his book: *'The Cygnus Mystery: Unlocking the Ancient Secret of Life's Origins in the Cosmos'*, its synopsis is:

> "It was a universal belief among ancient civilizations that life came originally from the cosmos, and ultimately would return there after death. The shamanic journey was always to this sky-world - and it appears that it was always located in the direction of the stars of Cygnus - also known as the Northern Cross - accessed either via the Milky Way or an imagined cosmic axis. Andrew Collins demonstrates that this belief is based on an ancient astronomy - around 17,000 years old. All over the world, standing stones, temples and monuments are orientated towards the rising and setting of the stars of the Cygnus constellation or the "entry point" of the Milky Way. Collins has discovered that the use of deep caves by Palaeolithic man was essential to the rise of religious thought and the belief in life's stellar origins..." [6]

Furthermore, Collins suggests the central axis of Avebury stone circle (circa 2000 BC) was aligned to the setting of the star Deneb in Cygnus. He also suggests Wayland's Smithy long barrow (circa 3700 BC) is aligned to the star Deneb in Cygnus, and the north face stone row of Callanish stone circle (circa 3000 BC) is aligned to the rising of Sadr in Cygnus. The Avebury and Deneb star link is interesting in helping to understand the various religious significances of this site.

Perhaps Andrew Collins' book and other examples highlight the importance of the Cygnus constellation, and now place the study of this constellation on top of the agenda of magicians.

PART OF AVEBURY STONE CIRCLE, PHOTO BY P. NABARZ.

PART OF AVEBURY STONE CIRCLE, PHOTO BY P. NABARZ.

CYGNUS RITE

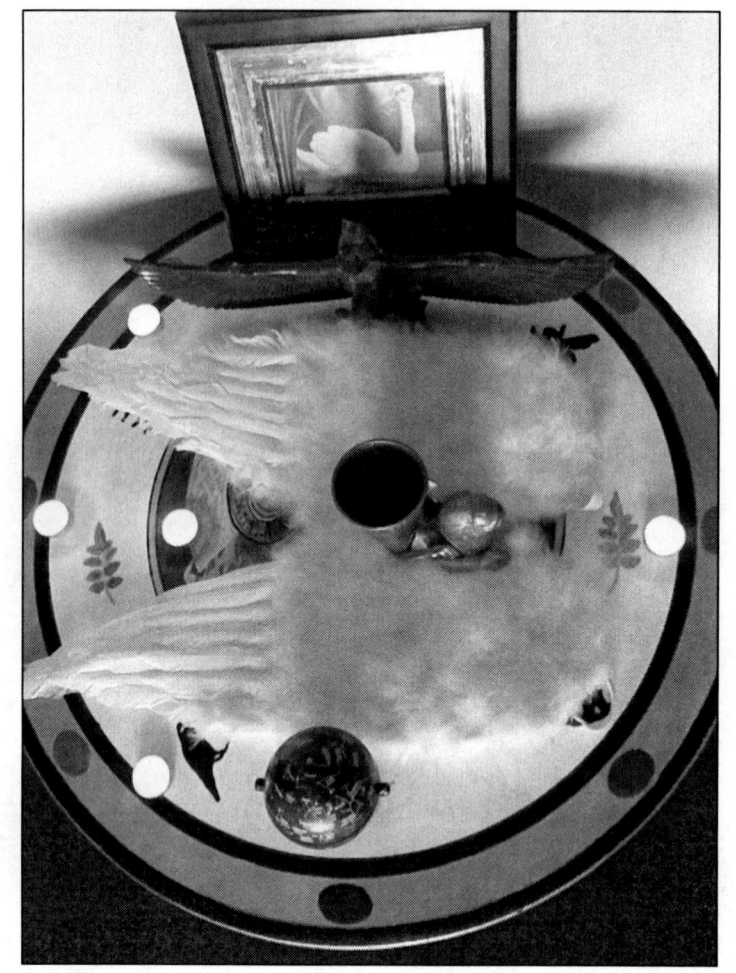

AN ALTAR TO CYGNUS, PHOTO BY P. NABARZ.

Set up

- ⊕ Location: a place with good visibility of stars. (If indoor with Stellar maps on altar).
- ⊕ Candles or tea lights to be lit and place on altar in shape of constellation Cygnus
- ⊕ Central fire lit (if needed due to cold) but kept to a size not to affect the night vision too much.

- ⊕ Time to perform this rite is determined using a Star-globe or Star-chart to ensure visibility of the Cygnus constellation.
- ⊕ Clothing: sensible outdoor clothing & footwear.
- ⊕ Altar cloth to have stars on it.
- ⊕ A Swan feather if possible.
- ⊕ Offerings
- ⊕ Face paint or body paint e.g. Henna or Woad or commercial ones from party shops.
- ⊕ Food and drink to share.

AN ALTAR TO CYGNUS, PHOTO BY P. NABARZ.

Use the body paint (e.g. Henna) to draw the stars of Cygnus (as large dots) on your body, in positions shown in usual pictures of Cygnus.

The standard opening mentioned in the chapter *'opening and closing of rites'* is used here. This is then followed by:
- ⊕ Light the candles which are set in the shape of the stars of the constellation Cygnus.
- ⊕ Declare your intent as wanting to connect to Cygnus and to *'draw down'* the power of Cygnus into yourself (if that is part of your intent).

- ⊕ While looking at the constellation, next take the stance of Cygnus, standing in the cross position arm raised at shoulder height.
- ⊕ Mediate on constellation Cygnus while standing in this position for few minutes.
- ⊕ When you feel ready read the following which is the summary version of the legend of Phaeton and Cygnus according to Ovid's *Metamorphosis*. It begins with Helios telling Phaeton about course of the suns journey in the heavens.
- ⊕ Before you start your reading visualise a door in front of you which has the stars of Cygnus painted on it.

"The first part of the road is steep, and such as the horses, though fresh in the morning, can hardly climb. In the middle of the heavens it is high aloft, from whence it is often a source of fear, even to myself, to look down upon the sea and the earth, and my breast trembles with fearful apprehensions. The last stage is a steep descent, and requires a sure command of the horses. Then, too, Tethys herself, who receives me in her waves, extended below, is often wont to fear, lest I should be borne headlong from above. Besides, the heavens are carried round with a constant rotation, and carry with them the lofty stars, and whirl them with rapid revolution. Against this I have to contend; and that force which overcomes all other things, does not overcome me; and I am carried in a contrary direction to the rapid world. Suppose the chariot given to thee; what couldst thou do? Couldst thou proceed, opposed to the whirling poles, so that the rapid heavens should not carry thee away? Perhaps, too, thou dost fancy in thy mind that there are groves, and cities of the Gods, and temples enriched with gifts: whereas, the way is through dangers, and the forms of wild beasts; and though thou shouldst keep on thy road, and be drawn aside by no wanderings, still thou must pass amid the horns of the threatening Bull, and the Hæmonian bow, and before the visage of the raging Lion, and the Scorpion, bending his cruel claws with a wide compass, and the Crab, that bends his claws in a different manner; nor is it easy for thee to govern the steeds spirited by those fires which they have in their breasts, and which they breathe forth from their mouths and their nostrils. Hardly are they restrained by me, when their high-mettled spirit is once heated, and their necks struggle against the reins.....
.... Soon as the steeds have perceived this, they rush on, and leave the beaten track, and run not in the order in which they did before. He himself becomes alarmed; and knows not which way to turn the reins entrusted to him, nor does he know where the way is, nor, if he did know, could he control them. Then, for

the first time, did the cold Triones grow warm with sunbeams, and attempt, in vain, to be dipped in the sea that was forbidden to them. And the Serpent which is situate next to the icy pole, being before torpid with cold, and formidable to no one, grew warm, and regained new rage from the heat. They say, too, that thou, Bootes, being disturbed, took to flight; although thou wast but slow, and thy wain impeded thee. But when, from the height of the skies, the unhappy Phaeton looked down upon the earth, lying far, very far beneath, he grew pale, and his knees shook with a sudden terror; and in a light so great, darkness overspread his eyes. And now he could wish that he had never touched the horses of his father; and now he is sorry that he knew his descent, and that he prevailed in his request; now desiring to be called the son of Merops. He is borne along, just as a ship driven by the furious Boreas, to which its pilot has given up the overpowered helm, and which he has resigned to the Gods and the effect of his supplications. What can he do? much of heaven is left behind his back; still more is before his eyes. Either space he measures in his mind; and at one moment he is looking forward to the West, which it is not allowed him by fate to reach; and sometimes he looks back upon the East. Ignorant what to do, he is stupefied; and he neither lets go the reins, nor is he able to retain them; nor does he know the names of the horses. In his fright, too, he sees strange objects scattered everywhere in various parts of the heavens, and the forms of huge wild beasts. There is a spot where the Scorpion bends his arms into two curves, and with his tail and claws bending on either side, he extends his limbs through the space of two signs of the Zodiac. As soon as the youth beheld him wet with the sweat of black venom, and threatening wounds with the barbed point of his tail, bereft of sense, he let go the reins, in a chill of horror. Soon as they, falling down, have touched the top of their backs, the horses range at large: and no one restraining them, they go through the air of an unknown region; and where their fury drives them thither, without check, do they hurry along, and they rush on to the stars fixed in the sky, and drag the chariot through pathless places....

... Jupiter, to save the universe from being consumed, hurls his thunder at Phaeton, on which he falls headlong into the river Eridanus and dies... The sisters of Phaeton are changed into poplars, and their tears become amber distilling from those trees...

Cycnus, the son of Sthenelus, was present at this strange event; who, although he was related to thee, Phaeton, on his mother's side, was yet more nearly allied in affection. He having left his kingdom (for he reigned over the people and the great cities of the Ligurians) was filling the verdant banks and the river Eridanus, and the wood, now augmented by the sisters, with his complaints; when the man's voice became shrill, and gray feathers concealed his hair. A long neck, too, extends from his breast, and a membrane joins his reddening toes; feathers

> *clothe his sides, and his mouth holds a bill without a point. Cycnus becomes a new bird; but he trusts himself not to the heavens or the air, as being mindful of the fire unjustly sent from thence. He frequents the pools and the wide lakes, and abhorring fire, he chooses the streams, the very contrary of flames."* [7]

The scorched path in the heavens from Phaeton journey is the Milky Way and the Cygnus still flies along it, its right wing stretched toward the right hand of the Cepheus constellation and its left wing toward the Pegasus constellation. The Eagle and Vulture fly near by, and the Vulture carries the harp of Orpheus, source of a magical music.

Sit down to meditate for a while on what has been said, a relevant music could be played to help with the meditation.

- ⊕ Saying of thanks to spirits of the place.
- ⊕ Final thanks to Cygnus, Phaeton, Eagle and Vulture (Lyra) and the Milky Way (Goddess Nuit).
- ⊕ The standard closing mentioned in the chapter *'opening and closing of rites'* is used here. This is followed by having something to eat and drink. Then Clear the space.

References

1. *Shah Nameh The Epic of Kings*, Ferdowsi, Abolqasem, translated by Helen Zimmern, 1883.
2. *The New Patterns in the Sky,* by Julius D.W. Staal 1988, McDonald & Woodward Publishing Company, p.175.
3. *The Penguin Dictionary of Symbols* by Jean Chevalier and Alain Gheerbrant, John Buchanan-Brown (Translator) (1969), New Edition 1996, p954.
4. *W.B. Yeats The Poems,* Edited by Daniel Albright, Dent, 1990. pp 550-551, p576, p663-665.
5. *Druid Renaissance: The Voice of Druidry Today,* Philip Carr-Gomm, Thorsons Publishers, 1996.
6. *The Cygnus Mystery: Unlocking the Ancient Secret of Life's Origins in the Cosmos' by* Andrew Collins, Watkins Publishing, 2007.
7. *The Metamorphoses of Ovid* Vol. I, Books I-VII Translator: Henry Thomas Riley, 1893.

Another translation available is: *The Metamorphoses of Ovid* translated into English verse under the direction of Sir Samuel Garth by John Dryden, Alexander Pope, Joseph Addison, William Congreve and other eminent hands, 1717.
Other translations include: May M. Innes, Penguin Classics (1955, New Edition 2002) and David Raeburn translation, Penguin Classics; New Ed edition (2004).

Further reading:
The Metamorphoses of Ovid translated by M. Innes, Penguin Classics (1955, New Edition 2002)
The Cygnus Mystery: Unlocking the Ancient Secret of Life's Origins in the Cosmos, Andrew Collins, Watkins Publishing, 2008.
Star Myths of the Greeks and Romans: A Sourcebook, by Theony Condos, Phanes Press, U.S, 1997.
Sun, Moon & Stars by Sheena McGrath, Capall Bann, 2005.

Notes:

THE PLEIADES

THE SEVEN SISTERS

PHOTO CREDIT: NASA, ESA AND AURA/CALTECH

INTRODUCTION

The bull slaying scene in the Mithraic Mysteries is a representation of the constellations of Perseus (Mithras), Taurus (bull), Canis Minor (dog), Hydra (snake), Corvus (raven), and Scorpio (scorpion). The wheat is the star Spica (the brightest star in the constellation Virgo) and where the knife enters the bull, it is the Pleiades; the life giving blood of the bull is the Milky Way.

The Pleiades are in the shoulder of Taurus and by the left foot of Perseus. According to Aratus' *Phaenomena* they are remembers as seven stars in songs, while only six are visible to the eye even though none has perished. They are called Halcyone, Merope, Celaeno, Electra, Sterope, Taygete and queenly Maia. They turn in heaven at morning and eventide to tell the beginning of summer and winter and the coming sowing season.

According to Thomas Bulfinch:

> *"The Pleiades were daughters of Atlas, and nymphs of Diana's train. One day Orion saw them and became enamoured and pursued them. In their distress they prayed to the gods to change their form, and Jupiter in pity turned them into pigeons, and then made them a constellation in the sky. Though their number was seven, only six stars are visible, for Electra, one of them, it is said left her place that she might not behold the ruin of Troy, for that city was founded by her son Dardanus. The*

sight had such an effect on her sisters that they have looked pale ever since."¹

The Pleiades are one of the most useful constellations in terms of seasonal markers. The rising and setting of Pleiades was an indicator for agriculture and seafaring. In Hesiod's *Works and Days* we read:

> "(ll. 383-404) When the Pleiades, daughters of Atlas, are rising (early in May), begin your harvest, and your ploughing when they are going to set (in November). Forty nights and days they are hidden and appear again as the year moves round, when first you sharpen your sickle. This is the law of the plains, and of those who live near the sea, and who inhabit rich country, the glens and dingles far from the tossing sea, -- strip to sow and strip to plough and strip to reap, if you wish to get in all Demeter's fruits in due season, and that each kind may grow in its season
>
> (ll. 609-617) But when Orion and Sirius are come into mid-heaven, and rosy-fingered Dawn sees Arcturus (September), then cut off all the grape-clusters, Perses, and bring them home. Show them to the sun ten days and ten nights: then cover them over for five, and on the sixth day draw off into vessels the gifts of joyful Dionysus. But when the Pleiades and Hyades and strong Orion begin to set (the end of October), then remember to plough in season: and so the completed year (that is, the succession of stars which make up the full year.) will fitly pass beneath the earth.
>
> (ll. 618-640) But if desire for uncomfortable sea-faring seize you; when the Pleiades plunge into the misty sea (The end of October or beginning of November) to escape Orion's rude strength, then truly gales of all kinds rage. Then keep ships no longer on the sparkling sea, but bethink you to till the land as I bid you. Haul up your ship upon the land and pack it closely with stones all round to keep off the power of the winds which blow damply, and draw out the bilge-plug so that the rain of heaven may not rot it. Put away all the tackle and fittings in your house, and stow the wings of the sea-going ship neatly, and hang up the well-shaped rudder over the smoke. You yourself wait until the season for sailing is come, and then haul your swift ship down to the sea and stow a convenient cargo in it, so that you may bring home profit, even as your father and mine, foolish Perses, used to sail on shipboard because he lacked sufficient livelihood."²

In the *Odyssey* we also read about sailing by the Pleiades:

> "Moreover, she made the wind fair and warm for him, and gladly did Ulysses spread his sail before it, while he sat and guided the raft skilfully by means of the rudder. He never closed his eyes, but kept them fixed on the Pleiades, on late-

setting Bootes, and on the Bear- which men also call the wain, and which turns round and round where it is, facing Orion, and alone never dipping into the stream of Oceanus - for Calypso had told him to keep this to his left. Days seven and ten did he sail over the sea, and on the eighteenth the dim outlines of the mountains on the nearest part of the Phaeacian coast appeared, rising like a shield on the horizon."[3]

In the Folk tales of some countries like Lithuania, it is said that the Pleiades follow the same path at night in the sky as the sun does in the sky during day time. This allowed people to use the movement of the Pleiades to tell the time at night in the same way position of sun was used at day time to tell the time.

The link between the Pleiades and water and Egyptian goddesses Hathor, Isis is one that I touch in the following piece:

Isis, Nuit, Hathor, Sol and the Ox

*"She has burst her banks,
She is very wet today;
Isis flows everywhere.
Isis is reaching for Nuit;
water levels rise higher.
Dawn arrives before the Sun's chariot,
Nuit is moved by her daughter - overnight labour.
She reaches down, clouds descend
haze engulfs the land of the Ox
and his partner Hathor.*

*Mist and river meet, sisterly gossip follows.
Swans and ducks swim where a week ago
the footballers played.
the ducks in the rugby field cheer
there are seven swans in the football pitch
paddling between the goal posts.
A feathered goal keeper
in the game of Isis v Ox.*

*There will be no Oxen fording today.
Bridges surrounded by water,
wooden islands with no visible paths
of entry or escape,
Footpaths, tow paths, deer tracks
all are submerged,
a highway for the fishes.*

*Only a single path remains,
one made by Man*

from stone, rock and sweat.
The path is just visible above the water line,
like a water snake swimming in the Isis.
Walking on this narrow path,
or is it walking on water?
Through the mists of Oxon.
Heading towards the dawn,
which appears at the end of the golden path.
Nuit leaves her daughter, mists disappear,
as the sun begins its daily journey across the sky;

but Isis keeps on rising up heavenward,
this time reaching for her lover; Sol.
Sol-Osiris too is reaching for her
with his penetrating rays.
His reflection is engulfed by her,
a fiery globe floating in the river of space,
together bringing nourishment to the land of the Ox.
It's going to be a beautiful day
on the Port Meadow sea front."
-Nabarz 10.2.07

An invocation from the *Greek Magical Papyri* can also be used here, this is an invocation to the holy angel Zizaubio who resides in the Pleiades. See PGM VII 795-845, the actual invocation is from line PGM VII.830 and starts with *"I call upon you, holy angel Zizaubio, from the company of the Pleiades to whom you are subordinate..."*[4]

PLEIADES RITE

Set up
- ⊕ Location: a place with good visibility of the stars. (If indoors with Stellar maps on the altar).
- ⊕ Seven Candles or tea lights to be lit and placed on altar in the shape of the constellation Pleiades
- ⊕ Central fire lit (if needed due to cold) but kept to a size not to affect the night vision too much.
- ⊕ Time to perform this rite is determined using a Star-globe or Star-chart to ensure the visibility of the Pleiades constellation.
- ⊕ Clothing: sensible outdoor clothing & footwear.
- ⊕ Altar cloth to have stars on it.
- ⊕ Offerings

⊕ Face paint or body paint e.g. Henna or Woad or commercial ones from party shops.
⊕ Food and drink to share.

AN ALTAR TO PLEIADES (PHOTO BY P. NABARZ).

Use the body paint (e.g. Henna) to draw the stars of the Pleiades (as large dots) on your body, in the positions shown in usual pictures of Pleiades.

The standard opening mentioned in the chapter *'opening and closing of rites'* is used here. This is then followed by:

Light the candles which are set in the shape of the stars of the constellation of Pleiades.

Declare your intent as wanting to connect to Pleiades and to *'draw down'* the power of Pleiades into yourself (if that is part of your intent).

While looking at the constellation, assume a relaxed stance, a position you are comfortable in.

Mediate on constellation Pleiades while standing in this position for a few minutes.

When you feel ready recite the following poem to Pleiades. Before you recite visualise a door in front of you which has the stars of Pleiades painted on it.

The Lost Pleiad

By William Gilmore Simms (1806–1870)

"Not in the sky,
Where it was seen
So long in eminence of light serene, -
Nor on the white tops of the glistering wave,
Nor down in mansions of the hidden deep,
Though beautiful in green
And crystal, its great caves of mystery, -
Shall the bright watcher have
Her place, and, as of old, high station keep!

Gone! gone!
Oh! nevermore, to cheer
The mariner, who holds his course alone
On the Atlantic, through the weary night,
When the stars turn to watchers, and do sleep,
Shall it again appear,
With the sweet-loving certainty of light,
Down shining on the shut eyes of the deep!

The upward-looking shepherd on the hills
Of Chaldea, night-returning with his flocks,
He wonders why his beauty doth not blaze,
Gladding his gaze, -
And, from his dreary watch along the rocks,
Guiding him homeward o'er the perilous ways!
How stands he waiting still, in a sad maze,
Much wondering, while the drowsy silence fills
The sorrowful vault! - how lingers, in the hope that night
May yet renew the expected and sweet light,
So natural to his sight!
And lone,
Where, at the first, in smiling love she shone,
Brood the once happy circle of bright stars:
How should they dream, until her fate was known,
That they were ever confiscate to death?
That dark oblivion the pure beauty mars,
And, like the earth, its common bloom and breath,
That they should fall from high;
Their lights grow blasted by a touch, and die,
All their concerted springs of harmony
Snapt rudely, and the generous music gone!

Ah! still the strain
Of wailing sweetness fills the saddening sky;
The sister stars, lamenting in their pain
That one of the selectest ones must die, -
Must vanish, when most lovely, from the rest!

*Alas! 't is ever thus the destiny.
Even Rapture's song hath evermore a tone
Of wailing, as for bliss too quickly gone.
The hope most precious is the soonest lost,
The flower most sweet is first to feel the frost.
Are not all short-lived things the loveliest?
And, like the pale star, shooting down the sky,
Look they not ever brightest, as they fly
From the lone sphere they blest!"[5]*

Next recite the actual invocation from PGM VII 829-841 which starts with *"I call upon you, holy angel Zizaubio, from the company of the Pleiades to whom you are subordinate... reveal all things to me through dreams with accuracy, O angel Zizaubio."*[4]

Another additional poem that can also be recited is the following section of **The Culprit Fay** by Joseph Rodman Drake (1795-1820).

*"I.
Tis the middle watch of a summer's night -
The earth is dark, but the heavens are bright;
Nought is seen in the vault on high
But the moon, and the stars, and the cloudless sky,
And the flood which rolls its milky hue,
A river of light on the welkin blue.
The moon looks down on old Cronest,
She mellows the shades on his shaggy breast,
And seems his huge gray form to throw
In a sliver cone on the wave below;*

*His sides are broken by spots of shade,
By the walnut bough and the cedar made,
And through their clustering branches dark
Glimmers and dies the fire-fly's spark -
Like starry twinkles that momently break
Through the rifts of the gathering tempest's rack.*

*II.
The stars are on the moving stream,
And fling, as its ripples gently flow,
A burnished length of wavy beam
In an eel-like, spiral line below;
The winds are whist, and the owl is still,
The bat in the shelvy rock is hid,
And nought is heard on the lonely hill
But the cricket's chirp, and the answer shrill
Of the gauze-winged katy-did;
And the plaint of the wailing whip-poor-will,
Who moans unseen, and ceaseless sings,
Ever a note of wail and wo,*

Till morning spreads her rosy wings,
And earth and sky in her glances glow.

III.

Tis the hour of fairy ban and spell:
The wood-tick has kept the minutes well;
He has counted them all with click and stroke,
Deep in the heart of the mountain oak,
And he has awakened the sentry elve
Who sleeps with him in the haunted tree,
To bid him ring the hour of twelve,
And call the fays to their revelry;
Twelve small strokes on his tinkling bell -
That was made of the white snail's pearly shell
Midnight comes, and all is well!
Hither, hither, wing your way!
This the dawn of the fairy day.
...

XXXII.
She raised her eyes to the wondering sprite,
And they leapt with smiles, for well I ween
Never before in the bowers of light
Had the form of an earthly Fay been seen.
Long she looked in his tiny face;
Long with his butterfly cloak she played;
She smoothed his wings of azure lace,
And handled the tassel of his blade;
And as he told in accents low
The story of his love and wo,
She felt new pains in her bosom rise,
And the tear-drop started in her eyes.
And 'O sweet spirit of earth,' she cried,
'Return no more to your woodland height,
But ever here with me abide
In the land of everlasting light!
Within the fleecy drift we'll lie,
We'll hang upon the rainbow's rim;
And all the jewels of the sky
Around thy brow shall brightly beam!
And thou shalt bathe thee in the stream
That rolls its whitening foam aboon,
And ride upon the lightning's gleam,
And dance upon the orbed moon!
We'll sit within the Pleiad ring,
We'll rest on Orion's starry belt,
And I will bid my sylphs to sing
The song that makes the dew-mist melt;
Their harps are of the umber shade,
That hides the blush of waking day,

*And every gleamy string is made
Of silvery moonshine's lengthened ray;
And thou shalt pillow on my breast,
While heavenly breathings float around,
And, with the sylphs of ether blest,
Forget the joys of fairy ground...*"[6]

Sit down to meditate for a while on what has been said, relevant music could be played to help with the meditation.

⊕ Saying of thanks to spirits of the place.
⊕ Final thanks to Pleiades.

The standard closing mentioned in the chapter *'opening and closing of rites'* is used here. This is followed by having something to eat and drink. Then clear the space.

References
1. *Bulfinch's mythology the age of fable or stories of gods and heroes* by Thomas Bulfinch, 1855.
2. *Works And Days* by Hesiod translated by Hugh G. Evelyn-White, 1914.
3. Book V, *The Odyssey* by Homer translated by Samuel Butler, 1900.
4. *The Greek Magical Papyri in Translation: Including the Demotic Spells*, Hans Dieter Betz, University Of Chicago Press, 1997, pp140-141.
5. *The Lost Pleiad* by William Gilmore Simms (1806-1870).
6. *The Culprit Fay* by Joseph Rodman Drake, (1795-1820).

Further NASA images of Pleiades:
http://hubblesite.org/newscenter/archive/releases/2004/20/image/a/

Further reading:
Star Myths of the Greeks and Romans: A Sourcebook, by Theony Condos, Phanes Press, U.S, 1997.
Sun, Moon & Stars by Sheena McGrath, Capall Bann, 2005.

For a very different view on Pleiades influences see:
The Pleiadian Agenda: A New Cosmology for the Age of Light, Barbara Hand Clow, Bear & Company, 1995.
The Family of Light: Pleiadian Tales and Lessons in Living by Barbara Marciniak, Bear & Company, 1998.
The Pleiadian Workbook: Awakening Your Divine Karma by Amorah Quan-Yin, Bear & Company, 1995.

Notes:

GREAT BEAR & LITTLE BEAR

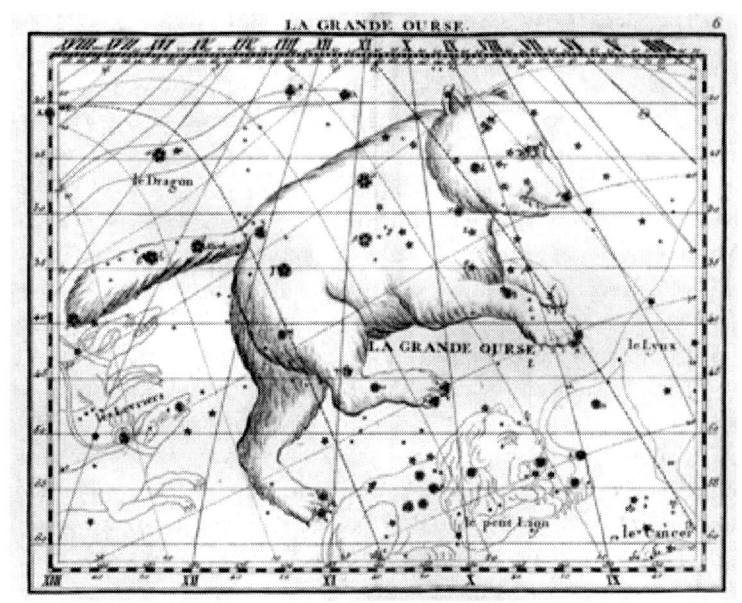

ATLAS CÉLESTE DE FLAMSTÉED

INTRODUCTION

> "Bear, Bear, you who rule the heaven, the stars, and the whole world; you who make the axis turn and control the whole cosmic system by force and compulsion...' PGM VII 686-690." [1]

In Sufism the constellation Bear appears numerous times. For example, the Persian Sufi Jami called his great work: *'The seven stars of the Great Bear'* or *Ruzbehan of Shiraz* saying:

> "I concentrated my attention on the constellation Bear (Ursa Minor) and I observed that it formed seven apertures through which God was showing himself to me. My God! I cried, what is this? He said to me: 'These are the seven apertures of the Throne. . . .' Every night, I continued afterward to observe these apertures in Heaven, as my love and ardent desire impelled me to do. And lo! One night, I saw that they were open, and I saw the divine Being manifesting to me through these apertures. He said to me, 'I manifest to you through these openings; they form

> seven thousand thresholds (corresponding to seven principal stars of the constellation) leading to the threshold of the angelic pleroma (malakut). And behold I show myself to you through all of them at once.'" -'Visions of the Pole, in the Sufi Ruzbehan of Shiraz, 1209.[2]

The Great Bear is one of the oldest constellations described by man; the Wagon is one of the constellations in the Babylonian *A Prayer to Gods of the Night* (circa 1700 BC). According to Aratus' *Phaenomena* (circa 270 BC) the two Bears surround the Pole and are referred to as the Wains. They face each other's flank and move along on all fours. Zeus willed the Bears to enter heaven from where they lived in Crete to show his gratitude, as when Zeus was a child in Dicton, they look after him for a year in their bear cave. On a very practical level, Greek and Phoenician sailors navigated by the Great Bear as it was easy to see; and it was by guidance of the Little Bear that the Phoenicians steered a straight course.

The Great Bear was seen in many different forms in various cultures, it was seen as the seven ploughing Oxen by the Romans, the Wagon by the Babylonians, the Plough in northwest Europe, Leg of the bull by the Egyptians, a Camel in North Africa, a shark in the East Indies and as the Bushel by the Chinese to name a few. The little Bear also goes by many names and shapes; it was seen as a Hippopotamus by the Egyptians, the lesser Wagon by the Babylonians, and a hunting horn by the Spanish.[3] The Welsh called the Great Bear *Cerbyd Arthur* which means 'Arthur's Wain'.[4] One suggestion is that Arthur translates as *'ar-taur - the one before the bull'*, in allusion to the god's depiction in the circumpolar stars standing before the heavenly bull Tarvos Trigaranus.'[5] Indeed Arthur means Bear, perhaps then the name 'Arthur Pendragon' which means Bear son of Dragon refers to the relationship of the Great Bear constellation and Draco constellation!

There are several Great Bear spells and charms in the *Greek Magical Papyri in Translation: Including the Demotic Spells*[1] these can be found in PGM VII 686-702, PGM IV 1275-1322, PGM VII 862, PGM XII 190, XIIb 26, and PGM LXXII. The Great Bear also appears in PGM in the Mithras Liturgy. I have already covered in depth the use of Mithraic Liturgy in my previous book (*The Mysteries of Mithras The Pagan Belief That Shaped the Christian World,* chapter 6) and will suggest you refer to that chapter for the details. That chapter provided a suggestion of how to work with the Bear and Pleiades constellations in conjunction. The approach taken was to use fourteen candles - seven white and seven black, in what can be described as seven brothers for seven sisters! Arrange the seven black candles on the left of the altar in the shape of the seven stars of the Plough constellation. On the right of the altar, arrange the seven white candles in shape of the Pleiades constellation. The seven white candles represent the seven Fates or Virgins that are part of the rite. The seven black candles represent the seven Black Bulls or Pole Lords, which are also part of the rite. The seven Fates, which have been described as having the faces of asps have been suggested by one scholar (Gundel) to be the seven Hathors (the Egyptian cow head goddesses). This puts forward the interesting vision that the magus, during his ascent in the rite, flies through a corridor or choir of seven black bulls (male) facing seven white cows (female). Mithras descends from the realm of the gods, or the eighth gate, to meet the ascending magus within this sacred bovine conduit, which suggests an additional meaning to the Mithras-Bull symbology.

It is also recommended that you read the chapter entitled *'North'* in *'Tankhem: meditations on Seth Magick'* by Mogg Morgan (Mandrake, 2003) and the chapter *'Deities attending the Northern Constellations'* in *Supernatural Assault in Ancient Egypt: Seth, Renpet and Moon Magick* by Mogg Morgan (Mandrake, 2008) where a great deal of information and insights into this constellation are provided.

The PGM VII.686-702 has already been incorporated into a modern ritual in *Hermetic Magic: The Postmodern Magickal Papyrus of Abaris*, by Stephen Edred Flowers, (Red Wheel/Weiser, 1995) pp200-201. Furthermore, PGM IV.1275-1322, has also been incorporated into a modern ritual in *Tankhem: mediations on Seth Magick* by Mogg Morgan (Mandrake, 2003) pp159-162. PGM based ceremonies to the Great Bear are well covered in these works; hence my focus here in this chapter and its rite will be on Ovid's tale of the *Great Bear and the Little Bear*.

For identifying stars in the night sky, locating the plough, the seven stars of the Ursa Major (Great Bear) that looks like a *'milk-pan'* is a key step. From the end two stars of the plough (Merak and Debhe) following an imaginary line straight upward will result in locating Polaris, the North Star. Polaris is in the tail of the constellation of Ursa Minor. Around Ursa Minor is the constellation Draco. If you follow in an arc the handle of the pan (Plough) or the tail of Ursa Major, this will lead to the star Arcturus (Guardian of the Bear), which is part of the Bootes constellation. If you continue the arc it will reach the star Spica in the constellation Virgo. If you follow the two middle stars of the Plough down it will reach the Leo Minor constellation and then the Leo Major constellation. If you follow the two diagonal stars toward the front paws of the Bear you reach Gemini, the twins Castor and Pollux.

A recent example of aligning buildings to the stars can be seen near the Greenwich Royal Observatory, the birth place of Greenwich Mean Time. The Greenwich Meridian (Prime Meridian or Longitude Zero degrees) marks the starting point of every time zone in the World. Here a group of six trees and a sun dial are placed in the shape of Ursa Minor, the sun dial as part of the tree complex represents the pole star (see photos) and sits on the Prime Meridian. This is an excellent example of *'as above, as below'*. The pole star is part of the *axis mundi* and the tip of the cosmic axis; world axis, the sculpture symbolically unites the cosmic axis with the Prime Meridian! The archaeoastronomists of the future will probably compare this site to other stellar sites.

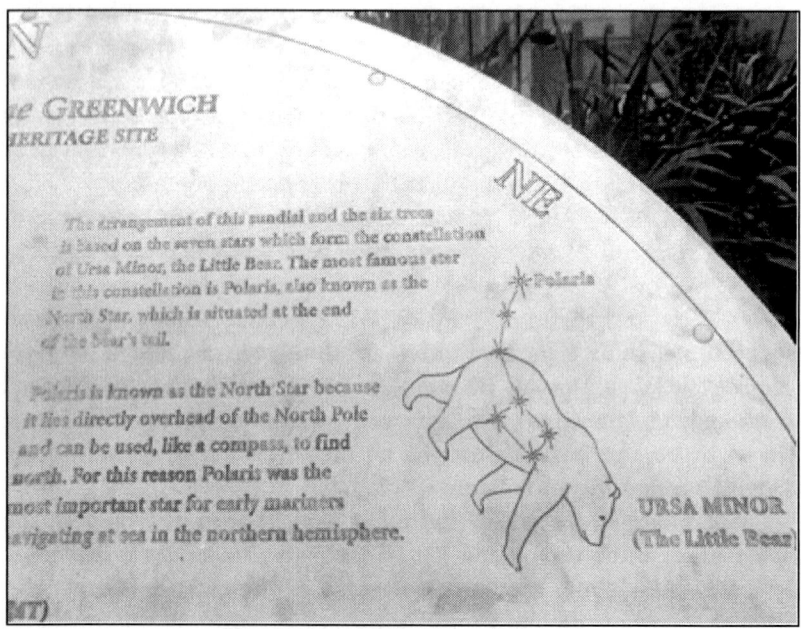

(URSA MINOR AT GMT, PHOTO BY P. NABARZ)

(Ursa Minor at GMT, photo by P. Nabarz)

(Ursa Minor at GMT, photo by P. Nabarz)

The myth behind the naming of the Great Bear according to Thomas Bulfinch is:

> *"Callisto was another maiden who excited the jealousy of Juno, and the goddess changed her into a bear. 'I will take away,' said she, 'that beauty with which you have captivated my husband.' Down fell Callisto on her hands and knees; she tried to stretch out her arms in supplication- they were already beginning to be covered with black hair. Her hands grew rounded, became armed with crooked claws, and served for feet; her mouth, which Jove used to praise for its beauty, became a horrid pair of jaws; her voice, which if unchanged would have moved the heart to pity, became a growl, more fit to inspire terror. Yet her former disposition remained, and with continual groaning, she bemoaned her fate, and stood upright as well as she could, lifting up her paws to be, for mercy, and felt that Jove was unkind, though she could not tell him so. Ah, how often, afraid to stay in the woods all night alone, she wandered about the neighbourhood of her former haunts; how often, frightened by the dogs, did she, so lately a huntress, fly in terror from the hunters! Often she fled from the wild beasts, forgetting that she was now a wild beast herself; and, bear as she was, was afraid of the bears.*
>
> *One day a youth espied her as he was hunting. She saw him and recognized him as her own son, now grown a young man. She stopped and felt inclined to embrace him. As she was about to approach, he, alarmed, raised his hunting spear, and was on the point of transfixing her, when Jupiter, beholding, arrested the crime, and snatching, away both of them, placed them in the heavens as the Great and Little Bear.*
>
> *Juno was in a rage to see her rival so set in honour, and hastened to ancient Tethys and Oceanus, the powers of ocean, and in answer to their inquiries thus told the cause of her coming: 'Do you ask why I, the queen of the gods, have left the heavenly plains and sought your depths? Learn that I am supplanted in heaven- my place is given to another. You will hardly believe me; but look when night darkens the world, and you shall see the two of whom I have so much reason to complain exalted to the heavens, in that part where the circle is the smallest, in the neighbourhood of the pole. Why should any one hereafter tremble at the thought of offending Juno when such rewards are the consequence of my displeasure? See what I have been able to effect! I forbade her to wear the human form- she is placed among the stars! So do my punishments result- such is the extent of my power! Better that she should have resumed her former shape, as I permitted Io to do. Perhaps he means to marry her, and put me away! But you, my foster-parents, if you feel for me, and see with displeasure this unworthy treatment of me, show it, I beseech you, by forbidding this couple from coming into your waters.' The powers of the ocean assented and consequently the two constellations of the*

Great and Little Bear move round and round in heaven, but never sink, as the other stars do, beneath the ocean."[6]

Thomas Bulfinch furthermore provides examples from Milton's poetry which linked to Great Bear: Milton alludes to the fact that the constellation of the Bear never sets, when he says:

> *"Let my lamp at midnight hour*
> *Be seen in some high lonely tower,*
> *Where I may oft outwatch the Bear."*

And Prometheus, in J. R. Lowell's poem, says:

> *"One after one the stars have risen and set,*
> *Sparkling upon the hoar frost of my chain;*
> *The Bear that prowled all night about the fold*
> *Of the North-star, hath shrunk into his den,*
> *Scared by the blithesome footsteps of the Dawn."*

The last star in the tail of the Little Bear is the Polestar, also called the Cynosure. Milton says:

> *"Straight mine eye hath caught new pleasures*
> *While the landscape round it measures.*
> *Towers and battlements it sees*
> *Bosomed high in tufted trees,*
> *Where perhaps some beauty lies*
> *The Cynosure of neighbouring eyes."*

The reference here is both to the Polestar as the guide of mariners, and to the magnetic attraction of the North. He calls it also the *'Star of Arcady,'* because Callisto's boy was named Arcas, and they lived in Arcadia. In Milton's' work *Comus*, the brother, benighted in the woods, says:

> *"...Some gentle taper!*
> *Though a rush candle, from the wicker hole*
> *Of some clay habitation, visit us*
> *With thy long levelled rule of streaming light,*
> *And thou shalt be our star of Arcady,*
> *Or Tyrian Cynosure."*[6]

GREAT BEAR RITE

AN ALTAR TO THE GREAT BEAR (PHOTO BY P. NABARZ)

Set up

- Location: a place with good visibility of stars. (If indoor with Stellar maps on altar).
- Candles or tea lights to be lit and place on altar in the shape of the constellation of the Great Bear
- Central fire lit (if needed due to cold) but kept to a size not to affect the night vision too much.
- Time to perform this rite is determined using a Star-globe or Star-chart to ensure visibility of the Great Bear constellation.
- Clothing: sensible outdoor clothing & footwear.
- Altar cloth to have stars on it.
- A bear photo or drawing.
- Offerings.
- Face paint or body paint e.g. Henna or Woad or commercial ones from party shops.
- Food and drink to share.

Use the body paint (e.g. Henna) to draw the stars of the Great Bear (as large dots) on your body, in positions shown in usual pictures of the Great Bear.

The standard opening mentioned in the chapter *'opening and closing of rites'* is used here. This is then followed by:

Light the candles which are set in shape of stars of the constellation of the Great Bear.

Declare your intent as wanting to connect to the Great Bear and the Little Bear and to *'draw down'* the power of the Great Bear into yourself (if that is part of your intent).

While looking at the constellation, next take the stance of a bear, standing up with arms raised, like a bear standing on its back legs and its paws raised above its head.

Mediate on the constellation of the Great Bear while standing in this position for few minutes.

When you feel ready recite the following poem to the Great Bear from Ovid's *Metamorphoses*. Before you recite visualise a door in front of you which has the stars of the Great Bear painted on it opening.

> "The day was settled in its course; and Jove
> Walked the wide circuit of the Heavens above,
> To search if any cracks or flaws were made;
> But all was safe: the Earth he then surveyed,
> And cast an eye on every different coast,
> And every land; but on Arcadia most.
> Her fields he clothed, and cheered her blasted face
> With running fountains, and with springing grass.
> No tracks of Heaven's destructive fire remain,
> The fields and woods revive, and Nature smiles again.
> But as the God walked to and fro the Earth,
> And raised the plants, and gave the spring its birth,
> By chance a fair Arcadian nymph he viewed,
> And felt the lovely charmer in his blood.
> The nymph nor spun, nor dressed with artful pride,
> Her vest was gathered up, her hair was tied;
> Now in her hand a slender spear she bore,
> Now a light quiver on her shoulders wore;
> To chaste Diana from her youth inclined,
> The sprightly warriors of the wood she joined.
> Diana too the gentle huntress loved,
> Nor was there one of all the nymphs that roved
> O'er Maenalus, amid the maiden throng,
> More favoured once; but favour lasts not long.
> The sun now shone in all its strength, and drove
> The heated virgin panting to a grove;
> The grove around a grateful shadow cast:
> She dropt her arrows, and her bow unbraced;
> She flung her self on the cool grassy bed;
> And on the painted quiver raised her head,

Jove saw the charming huntress unprepared,
Stretched on the verdant turf, without a guard.
Here I am safe, he cries, from Juno's eye;
Or should my jealous queen the theft descry,
Yet would I venture on a theft like this,
And stand her rage for such, for such a bliss!
Diana's shape and habit strait he took,
Softened his brows, and smoothed his awful look,
And mildly in a female accent spoke.
How fares my girl? How went the morning chase?
To whom the virgin, starting from the grass,
All hail, bright deity, whom I prefer
To Jove himself, tho' Jove himself were here.
The God was nearer than she thought, and heard
Well-pleased himself before himself preferred.
He then salutes her with a warm embrace;
And, e're she half had told the morning chase,
With love enflamed, and eager on his bliss,
Smothered her words, and stopped her with a kiss;
His kisses with unwonted ardour glowed,
Nor could Diana's shape conceal the God.
The virgin did whatever a virgin could
(Sure Juno must have pardoned, had she viewed);
With all her might against his force she strove;
But how can mortal maids contend with Jove?
Possest at length of what his heart desired,
Back to his Heavens, the' exulting God retired.
The lovely huntress, rising from the grass,
With down-cast eyes, and with a blushing face,
By shame confounded, and by fear dismayed,
Flew from the covert of the guilty shade,
And almost, in the tumult of her mind,
Left her forgotten bow and shafts behind.
But now Diana, with a sprightly train
Of quivered virgins, bounding o'er the plain,
Called to the nymph; the nymph began to fear
A second fraud, a Jove disguised in her;
But, when she saw the sister nymphs, suppressed
Her rising fears, and mingled with the rest.
How in the look does conscious guilt appear!
Slowly she moved, and loitered in the rear;
Nor lightly tripped, nor by the Goddess ran,
As once she used, the foremost of the train.
Her looks were flushed, and sullen was her mien,
That sure the virgin Goddess (had she been
Aught but a virgin) must the guilt have seen.
This said the nymphs saw all, and guessed aright:
And now the moon had nine times lost her light,
When Dian, fainting in the mid-day beams,
Found a cool covert, and refreshing streams
That in soft murmurs through the forest flowed,

*And a smooth bed of shining gravel showed.
A covert so obscure, and streams so clear,
The Goddess praised: 'And now no spies are near
Let's strip, my gentle maids, and wash,' she cries.
Pleased with the motion, every maid complies;
Only the blushing huntress stood confused,
And formed delays, and her delays excused;
In vain excused: her fellows round her pressed,
And the reluctant nymph by force undressed,
The naked huntress all her shame revealed,
In vain her hands the pregnant womb concealed;
'Begone!' the Goddess cries with stern disdain,
'Begone! nor dare the hallowed stream to stain':
She fled, for ever banished from the train.
This Juno heard, who long had watched her time
To punish the detested rival's crime;
The time was come; for, to enrage her more,
A lovely boy the teeming rival bore.
The Goddess cast a furious look, and cried,
'It is enough! I'm fully satisfied!
This boy shall stand a living mark, to prove
My husband's baseness and the strumpet's love:
But vengeance shall awake: those guilty charms
That drew the Thunderer from Juno's arms,
No longer shall their wonted force retain,
Nor please the God, nor make the mortal vain.'
Swung her to Earth, and dragged her on the ground:
The prostrate wretch lifts up her arms in prayer;
Her arms grow shaggy, and deformed with hair,
Her nails are sharpened into pointed claws,
Her hands bear half her weight, and turn to paws;
Her lips, that once could tempt a God, begin
To grow distorted in an ugly grin.
And, lest the supplicating brute might reach
The ears of Jove, she was deprived of speech:
Her surly voice thro' a hoarse passage came
In savage sounds: her mind was still the same,
The furry monster fixed her eyes above,
And heav'd her new unwieldy paws to Jove,
And begged his aid with inward groans; and tho'
She could not call him false, she thought him so.
How did she fear to lodge in woods alone,
And haunt the fields and meadows, once her own!
How often would the deep-mouthed dogs pursue,
Whilst from her hounds the frighted huntress flew!
How did she fear her fellow-brutes, and shun
The shaggy bear, tho' now her self was one!
How from the sight of rugged wolves retire,
Although the grim Lycaon was her sire!
But now her son had fifteen summers told,
When, as he beat the woods in quest of prey,*

> *He chanced to rouse his mother where she lay.*
> *She knew her son, and kept him in her sight,*
> *And fondly gazed: the boy was in a fright,*
> *And aimed a pointed arrow at her breast,*
> *And would have slain his mother in the beast;*
> *But Jove forbad, and snatched 'em through the air*
> *In whirlwinds up to Heav'n, and fixed 'em there!*
> *Where the new constellations nightly rise,*
> *And add a lustre to the northern skies.*
> *When Juno saw the rival in her height,*
> *Spangled with stars, and circled round with light,*
> *She sought old Ocean in his deep abodes,*
> *And Tethys, both rever'd among the Gods.*
> *They ask what brings her there: Ne'er ask, says she,*
> *What brings me here, Heav'n is no place for me.*
> *You'll see, when night has covered all things o'er,*
> *Jove's starry bastard and triumphant whore*
> *Usurp the Heavens; you'll see 'em proudly rowle*
> *And who shall now on Juno's altars wait,*
> *When those she hates grow greater by her hate?*
> *I on the nymph a brutal form impressed,*
> *Jove to a goddess has transformed the beast;*
> *This, this was all my weak revenge could do:*
> *But let the God his chaste amours pursue,*
> *And, as he acted after Io's rape,*
> *Restore the' adulteress to her former shape;*
> *Then may he cast his Juno off, and lead*
> *The great Lycaon's offspring to his bed.*
> *But you, ye venerable Powers, be kind,*
> *And, if my wrongs a due resentment find,*
> *Receive not in your waves their setting beams,*
> *Nor let the glaring strumpet taint your streams.*
> *The Goddess ended, and her wish was given.*
> *Back she returned in triumph up to Heaven;*
> *Her gawdy peacocks drew her through the skies.*
> *Their tails were spotted with a thousand eyes;*
> *The eyes of Argus on their tails were ranged,*
> *At the same time the raven's colour changed."*[7]

Sit down to meditate for a while on what has been said, relevant music could be played to help with the meditation.

- ⊕ Saying of thanks to spirits of the place.
- ⊕ Final thanks to the Great Bear and the Little Bear.

The standard closing mentioned in the chapter *'opening and closing of rites'* is used here. This is followed by having something to eat and drink. Then clear the space.

References
1. *The Greek Magical Papyri in Translation: Including the Demotic Spells*, Hans Dieter Betz, University Of Chicago Press, 1997.
2. *The Man of Light in Iranian Sufism* by Henry Corbin, Omega Publications, 1994, pp52-55.
3. *The New Patterns in the Sky: Myths and Legends of the Stars*, Julius D.W. Staal, McDonald & Woodward Publishing Company, 1998, pp121-142.
4. *The Penguin Dictionary of Symbols,* John Buchanan-Brown, and Jean Chevalier, and Alain Gheerbrant, Penguin Books Ltd, 1986, p75 & p451.
5. *The Lost Zodiac of the Druids,* Gregory Clouter, Vega, 2003. p172.
6. *Bulfinch's mythology the age of fable or stories of gods and heroes* by Thomas Bulfinch, 1855.
7. Book two Story of Callisto in *Metamorphoses* by Ovid translated into English verse under the direction of Sir Samuel Garth by John Dryden, Alexander Pope, Joseph Addison, William Congreve and other eminent hands, 1717.

Another translation that is available is *The Metamorphoses* of Ovid Vol. I, Books I-VII Translator: Henry Thomas Riley, 1893.

Other translations include: May M. Innes, Penguin Classics (1955, New Edition 2002) and David Raeburn translation, Penguin Classics; New Ed edition (2004).

Further reading
Chapter 6 in *The Mysteries of Mithras The Pagan Belief That Shaped the Christian World,* by Payam Nabarz, Inner Traditions, 2005.

Chapter 'North' in *'Tankhem: mediations on Seth Magick'* by Mogg Morgan (Mandrake, 2003).

Chapter 'Deities attending the Northern Constellations' in *Supernatural Assault in Ancient Egypt: Seth, Renpet and Moon Magick* by Mogg Morgan (Mandrake, 2008)

Section 14. Bear working to Arktos (PGM 686-702) in Divine Invocation chapter in

Hermetic Magic: The Postmodern Magickal Papyrus of Abaris, by Stephen Edred Flowers, Red Wheel/Weiser, 1995, pp200-201.

Notes:

DRACO

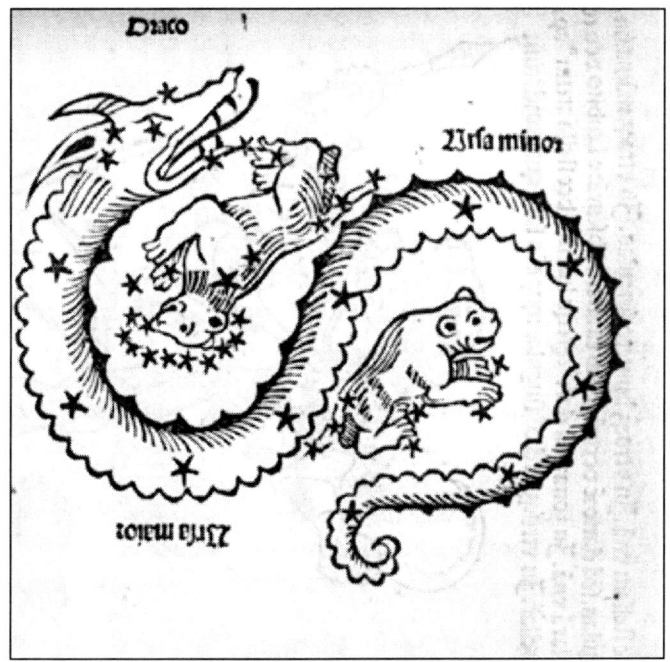

HYGINUS - POETICON ASTRONOMICON

INTRODUCTION

*"I am the Heart; and the Snake is entwined
About the invisible core of the mind.
Rise, O my snake! It is now is the hour
Of the hooded and holy ineffable flower.
Rise, O my snake, into brilliance of bloom...
... So also is the end of the book, and the Lord Adonai is about it on all sides like a Thunderbolt, and a Pylon, and a Snake, and a Phallus, and in the midst thereof he is like the Woman that jetteth out the milk of the stars from her paps; yea, the milk of the stars from her paps." - Liber Cordis Cincti Serpente vel LXV by Aleister Crowley*[1]

The importance of Draco in modern magic is illustrated by numerous magical groups who incorporate the current/names like Typhon, Draco, and Dragon in their group's names. The Draconian

155 | Stellar Magic

cults and groups according to the occult author Kenneth Grant go back to ancient Africa and Egypt. The topic of dragons and snakes is a vast subject and numerous books cover it. Grant's works *Cults of Shadow, Outer Gateways,* and *Outside the Circles of Time* all explore the Draco current in myriad of ways. However, before looking at the modern manifestation of the current we will examine the ancient tales.

According to Aratus' *Phaenomena,* between the two circumpolar Bears, like a river the Draco circles and winds around forever, the tail of Draco reaches toward one Bear and circles him while his head reaches toward the other. Two stars shine on the Draco's head and two stars in his eyes and one on his chin.

At 3000 BC the pole star was Draco's star Thuban (Alpha Draconis), and the Pharaoh Khufu's tomb, the largest pyramid in Egypt has a shaft aligned to it, while another shaft points to Orion's belt.

The dragon and snake are universal symbols and are seen in many cultures. In Hinduism the god Shiva is often shown with a snake (Vasuki) curled three times around his neck, there is also *'Anata'* meaning *'Endless, infinite'*; the name of the world snake on which the god Vishnu lies in his form as Anantasayana.

The Babylonian tale of the sea dragon goddess Tiamat being slain by the solar god Marduk is part of a creation story where from the body and flesh of the dragon humans are formed. Marduk defeats Tiamat by forcing wind down her throat so she could not close her mouth and then fired arrows down her throat killing her.

In the Persian version of the story, Âtar, the lord of fire and son of Ahura Mazda, attack the dragon Azi Dahâka. He tells the dragon:

> "There give it up to me, thou three-mouthed Azi Dahâka. If thou seizest that Glory that cannot be forcibly seized, then I will enter thy hinder part, I will blaze up in thy jaws, so that thou mayest never more rush upon the earth made by Mazda and destroy the world of the good principle." Yasht 19, 50. The Zend Avesta, Part II (SBE23), trans. James Darmesteter, (1882). [2]

The Persian dragon slayer is Thraêtaona who defeats Azi Dahâka by binding him and imprisoning him deep in a mountain top. To achieve this Thraêtaona makes many offerings to the goddess Drvâspa whose name means *'with solid horses'* and is probably linked to the sea goddess Anahita as they both share some characteristics. It is with the backing of the goddess Drvâspa that Thraêtaona wins against the dragon. In Yasht 9 we read:

> "To her (Drvâspa) did Thraêtaona, the heir of the valiant Âthwya clan, offer up a sacrifice in the four-cornered Varena,

> with a hundred male horses, a thousand oxen, ten thousand lambs, and with an offering of libations: 'Grant me this boon, O good, most beneficent Drvâspa! that I may overcome Azi Dahâka, the three-mouthed, the three-headed, the six-eyed, who has a thousand senses, that most powerful, fiendish Drug, that demon, baleful to the world, the strongest Drug that Angra Mainyu created against the material world, to destroy the world of the good principle; and that I may deliver his two wives, Savanghavâk and Erenavâk, who are the fairest of body amongst women, and the most wonderful creatures in the world.' The powerful Drvâspa, made by Mazda, the holy Drvâspa, the maintainer, granted him that boon, as he was offering up libations, giving gifts, sacrificing, and entreating that she would grant him that boon." Yasht 9, 13-15. The Zend Avesta, Part II (SBE23), trans. James Darmesteter, (1882).[3]

The dragon as a teacher and tester is seen in the story of King Feridoun and his three sons in the Persian Shah Nameh:

> "Now it came about that when Feridoun learned that his sons were returning, he went forth to meet them and prove their hearts. So he took upon him the form of a dragon that foamed at the mouth with fury, and from whose jaws sprang mighty flames. And when his sons were come near unto the mountain pass, he came upon them suddenly, like to a whirlwind, and raised a cloud of dust about the place with his writhings, and his roaring filled the air with noise. Then he threw himself upon the eldest born, and the prince laid down his spear and said, 'A wise and prudent man striveth not with dragons.' And he turned his back and fled before the monster, and left him to fall upon his brothers.
> Then the dragon sprang upon the second, and he said, 'An it be that I must fight, what matter if it be a furious lion or a knight full of valour?' So he took his bow and stretched it. But the youngest came towards him, and seeing the dragon, said, 'Thou reptile, flee from our presence, and strut not in the path of lions. For if thou hast heard the name of Feridoun, beware how thou doest thus, for we are his sons, armed with spears and ready for the fight. Quit therefore, I counsel thee, thine evil path, lest I plant upon thy head the crown of enmity. Then the glorious Feridoun, when he had thus made trial of their hearts, vanished from their sight. But presently he came again with the face of their father, and many warriors, elephants, and cymbals were in his train." The Epic of Kings by Ferdowsi, trans. Helen Zimmern (1883).[4]

On a more subtle esoteric level, Laleh Bakhtiar beautifully describes the mystical significance of the dragon in the Sufi way of understanding:

> "In Sufism the dragon relates two astronomical nodes, two diametrically opposed points of intersection between the moon and the sun. Its head is the ascending node, its tail the descending node. An eclipse can only occur when both sun and moon stand at the nodes. To the mystic, the dragon symbolizes the place of encounter between the moon and the sun within. The dragon can either devour the moon, seen symbolically as the mystic's spiritual heart, or it can serve as the place or container of conception. By entering the dragon when the sun is in the nodes, the moon or the heart conceives. Thus, in full consciousness of the perils, one must enter the dragon to await the eclipse in its cosmic womb." - Sufi Expressions of the Mystic Quest by Laleh Bakhtiar. [5]

A local dragon myth relevant to where I live now in Oxford is in the famous Welsh epic the *Mabinogion*, in story of King Lludd and Llevelys describes three plagues that had fallen upon the isle of Britain. One of these plagues was a scream that was heard:

> "a shriek which came on every May-Eve (Beltane), over every hearth in the Island of Britain. And this went through people's hearts, and so scared them, that the men lost their hue and their strength, and the women their children, and the young men and the maidens lost their senses, and all the animals and trees and the earth and the waters, were left barren.'. The cause of this plague was a foreign dragon fighting a local dragon. To overcome the dragon Lludd was told he had: 'the Island to be measured in its length and breadth, and in the place where thou dost find the exact central point, there cause a pit to be dug, and cause a cauldron full of the best mead that can be made to be put in the pit, with a covering of satin over the face of the cauldron. And then, in thine own person do thou remain there watching, and thou wilt see the dragon fighting in the form of terrific animals. And at length they will take the form of dragons in the air. And last of all, after wearying themselves with fierce and furious fighting, they will fall in the form of two pigs upon the covering, and they will sink in, and the covering with them, and they will draw it down to the very bottom of the cauldron. And they will drink up the whole of the mead; and after that they will sleep. Thereupon do thou immediately fold the covering around them, and bury them in a kistvaen (stone chest), in the strongest place thou hast in thy dominions, and hide them in the earth. And as long as they shall bide in that strong place no plague shall come to the Island of Britain from elsewhere." The Mabinogion by Lady Charlotte Guest, 1877. [6]

The alchemical symbol of the Ouroboros, a snake swallowing its own tail is said to represent the wheel of time, constantly renewing itself. Plato in *Timaeus*, also describes a circular, self contained snake like creature as the first created being. In Mithraism too, we see a snake curling around the body of the Mithraic *'God of Time'* the Leontocephaline, a figure often described as Immortal Time and Aion. The snake is also a symbol of Damballah, the Voodoo god of fertility. We see a central role for snakes in the Norse myths too; the world tree *Yggdrasil* had at its base a great cosmic serpent that gnawed at its roots while guarding it. This is Draco around the Pole star, here Yggdrasil like the Leontocephaline represents the Axis Mundi going through the Pole Star to other realms.

In Islamic Hadith, some snakes are described as Jinns (evil spirits); if someone sees a snake in their house, they should give it a warning three times over three days. If the snake returns after the warnings, they should kill it, for it is evil. Giving three warnings gives *'time'* to the snake to escape.

In the Mayan Calendar one of the twenty day names is that of the snake, while in Chinese Zodiac the snake is name of the one the 12 astrological years. Those born in year of the snake are seen as subtle, elusive, secretive, enigmatic and reliable.

The connection between the snake and time is seen in many mythologies, none more so than the Persian Zoroastrian *Mar Nameh: The Book of the Snake*. Here we see the battle between forces of Light (Ahura Mazda) and Darkness (Ahriman) is fought in *'Time'*. The twin sons of Zurvan (the Immortal Time) battle for dominion over the worlds.

For further discussion on esoteric importance of snakes see my book *The Persian 'Mar Nameh': The Zoroastrian 'Book of the Snake Omens* (Twin Serpents, 2006) and Jan Fries' book: *Seidways: Shaking, Swaying and Serpent Mysteries* (Mandrake, 1996).

For the purpose of this chapter on Draco, the focus will be limited mainly to the constellation the Draco within Greek and the Roman manifestation of the current.

In one story, Draco is Typhon, who fought Athena during the war of the Titans with the younger gods. In the heat of battle Athena, being a strategist and a goddess of wisdom, grabs Typhon by his tail and throws him into the stars, where it became fixed by the pole of star. The twisted Typhon is around the pole of heaven, where it is cold and unable to move. In the story of Phaeton he comes near and warms the frozen dragon causing him to start moving slightly again.

In another story the constellation Draco is the serpent Ladon which guarded the golden apples of Hesperides (Little Bear) and was placed in that role by the goddess Hera. After it was slain by Heracles it was place among the stars. The constellation Heracles lies above Draco and was placed there by Zeus as a token of the great battle that took place between Heracles and Draco. Another variation to the story according to Thomas Bulfinch is:

> "The most difficult labour of all was getting the golden apples of the Hesperides, for Hercules did not know where to find them. These were the apples which Juno had received at her wedding from the goddess of the Earth, and which she had in-trusted to the keeping of the daughters of Hesperus, assisted by a watchful dragon. After various adventures Hercules arrived at Mount Atlas in Africa. Atlas was one of the Titans who had warred against the gods, and after they were subdued, Atlas was condemned to bear on his shoulders the weight of the heavens. He was the father of the Hesperides, and Hercules thought might, if anyone could, find the apples and bring them to him. But how to send Atlas away from his post, or bear up the heavens while he was gone? Hercules took the burden on his own shoulders, and sent Atlas to seek the apples. He returned with them, and though somewhat reluctantly, took his burden upon his shoulders again, and let Hercules return with the apples to Eurystheus." Bulfinch's mythology the age of fable or stories of gods and heroes by Thomas Bulfinch, (1855).[7]

Thomas Bulfinch further points to Milton in his writing:

> "Milton, in his Comus, makes the Hesperides the daughters of Hesperus and niece of Atlas:
>> '...amidst the gardens fair
>> Of Hesperus and his daughters three,
>> That sing about the golden tree.'"
>
> "The poets, led by the analogy of the lovely appearance of the western sky at sunset, viewed the west as a region of brightness and glory. Hence they placed in it the Isles of the Blest, the ruddy Isle Erytheia, on which the bright oxen of Geryon were pastured, and the Isle of the Hesperides. The apples are supposed by some to be the oranges of Spain, of which the Greeks had heard some obscure accounts." Bulfinch's mythology: the age of fable or stories of gods and heroes by Thomas Bulfinch, (1855).[7]

DRACO RITE

A DRACO ALTAR (PHOTO BY P. NABARZ).

Set up

- ⊕ Location: a place with good visibility of stars. (If indoor with Stellar maps on altar).
- ⊕ Candles or tea lights to be lit and place on altar in shape of constellation Draco.
- ⊕ Central fire lit (if needed due to cold) but kept to a size not to affect the night vision too much.
- ⊕ Time to perform this rite is determined using a Star-globe or Star-chart to ensure visibility of the Draco constellation.
- ⊕ Clothing: sensible outdoor clothing & footwear.
- ⊕ Altar cloth to have stars on it.
- ⊕ Offerings.

- Face paint or body paint e.g. Henna or Woad or commercial ones from party shops.
- Food and drink to share.

Use the body paint (e.g. Henna) to draw the stars of Draco (as large dots) on your body, in positions shown in usual pictures of Draco.

The standard opening mentioned in the chapter *'opening and closing of rites'* is used here. This is then followed by:

Light the candles which are set in shape of stars of constellation Draco.

Declare your intent as wanting to connect with Draco and to *'draw down'* the power of Draco into yourself (if that is part of your intent).

While looking at the constellation, next take the stance of Draco, standing with your arm above you so your body is in the shape of an S.

Mediate on the constellation of Draco while standing in this position for few minutes.

When you feel ready there, visualise a door in front of you which has the stars of Draco painted on it. Before you proceed to the door, there is a choice for the next stage depending on your personal preferences.

A) You can recite Aleister Crowley's *Liber LXV* (*Liber Cordis Cincti Serpente, 'The Book of the Heart Girt with a Serpent'*)[8] to Draco. Then sit down to meditate for a while on what has been said, relevant music could be played to help with the meditation.

or B) You can use the Nordic seething technique as described in chapter 11 of Jan Fries book: *'Seidways: Shaking, Swaying and Serpent Mysteries'* (Mandrake, 1996).[9] My own preference is the seething option, to do this the dragon version of the seething method is used as described on pages 131-132 of *Seidways*. This technique allows you to draw into yourself the energy of the earth dragon from below and energy of sky dragon from above.

Once you feel connected to the dragon current using either the Liber LXV recitation approach or seething dragon approach, visualize the door with the stars of Draco painted on it open and enter the dragon.

How you would interact with the dragon is up to you! There are many manifestations of Draco through the ages, what is its mystery?

Will you try to get past the dragon and grab a golden apple?

How will you get pass the dragon? Do you need to:
Use force like St. George? and slay the dragon?
Or by cunning, like Hercules getting Atlas to steal an apple for you?
Or will you offer a trade and exchange?
Or will you offer an alliance?
Or will you try to seduce the dragon and become its lover?
Or will you offer yourself like as a 'virgin' to win its favour?
Or will you turn back now?

Draco protects its wisdom, and he is wrapped around the treasure chest that is the pole star. How you obtain its wisdom is an indication of who you are and what type of person you are. This is one of the many insights Draco can offer you.

Sit down to meditate for a while on how you will get pass the dragon guarding its treasures, a relevant music could be played to help with the meditation.

⊕ Saying of thanks to spirits of the place.
⊕ Final thanks to Draco.

The standard closing mentioned in the chapter *'opening and closing of rites'* is used here. This is followed by having something to eat and drink. Clear the space.

References

1. *Liber LXV* (Liber Cordis Cincti Serpente, "The Book of the Heart Girt with a Serpent") by Aleister Crowley.
2. *Yasht 19, 50. The Zend Avesta, Part II (SBE23),* James Darmesteter, translator, 1882.
3. *Yasht 9, 13-15. The Zend Avesta, Part II (SBE23),* James Darmesteter, translator, 1882.
4. *Shah Nameh The Epic of Kings* by Ferdowsi Translated by Helen Zimmern, 1883.
5. *Sufi Expressions of the Mystic Quest* by Laleh Bakhtiar, Thames and Hudson 1997, p45.
6. *The Mabinogion* by Lady Charlotte Guest, 1877.
7. *Bulfinch's mythology the age of fable or stories of gods and heroes* by Thomas Bulfinch, (1855).
8. *Liber LXV (Liber Cordis Cincti Serpente, "The Book of the Heart Girt with a Serpent")* by Aleister Crowley.
9. *Seidways: shaking, swaying and serpent mysteries'* by Jan Fries, Mandrake, 1996, p131-132.

Notes:

Twelve Signs
of the Zodiac

Mithras Kosmokrator/ Phanes. (From *The Mysteries of Mithra*, by Franz Cumont, 1956.

Introduction

"I passed the confines of death, treading the threshold of Proserpina, and returned having passed through all the elements. In the middle of the night I saw the sun flashing with bright light, and I met the gods beneath and above, and worshipped before them."- Metamorphoses, Lucius Apuleius.

The most popular form of stellar lore is general awareness of one's birth sun sign. Many newspapers provide daily horoscopes and there are numerous books and magazine covering the divinatory aspect of the twelve signs of Zodiac. However, this popular form is only the tip of the iceberg of the magical lore of the Zodiac. There are numerous associated myths to the Zodiac such as the twelve labours of Hercules seen as the sun's passage through the sign of the Zodiac; the journey of Jason and the Argonauts representing the sun's voyage through the Zodiac; or other links like the twelve tribes of Israel; the twelve Apostles; King Arthur and his twelve Knights of the Round Table; to name a few.

There are other applications for the twelve signs of the Zodiac, for examples they have been used in the astrological memory art, which is a version of theatre of memory. The Greek poet Metrodorus of Scepsis used the twelve constellations of the zodiac, which where subdivided into 360 separate storage places.[1]

An intriguing use of the Zodiac was in Melothesia or astrological medicine which assigns planet and zodiacal signs to body parts! The treatment would be aligned to position of the stars. One part of the body is to one sign:

- ⊕ Aries - Ram - Head
- ⊕ Gemini - Twins - arms
- ⊕ Leo - Lion - heart
- ⊕ Libra - Scales - Pelvis
- ⊕ Sagittarius - Man Horse - Thighs
- ⊕ Aquarius - Waterman - Lower leg
- ⊕ Taurus - Bull - Neck and Throat
- ⊕ Cancer - Crab - Chest and Breasts
- ⊕ Virgo - Virgin - Womb
- ⊕ Scorpio - Scorpion - Sexual Parts
- ⊕ Capricorn - Goat Fish – Knees
- ⊕ Pisces - Fishes – Feet

The role of the signs of the Zodiac in Kabbalah provides a highly useful template for Zodiac based rites. The four principal Tribes of Israel are linked to constellations. According to John P. Pratt:

> *"Jacob (Israel) had twelve sons, and each of them is associated in Hebrew tradition with one of the twelve constellations of the zodiac. Hebrew scholars are not sure of the correspondence of all twelve, but the identities of the four which refer to the royal constellations are clear from the scriptures. They are the four principal tribes: Reuben, Judah, Dan, and Joseph."*[2]

The cube of space is seen in the classic second century CE Kabbalistic text *Sefer Yetzirah*[3], here the twelve simple Hebrew letters represent the twelve signs of the Zodiac. The letters are placed on a cube, and each sign ends up exactly opposite the sign (letter) which is opposite it in the usual Zodiac circular display.[3,4,5,6]

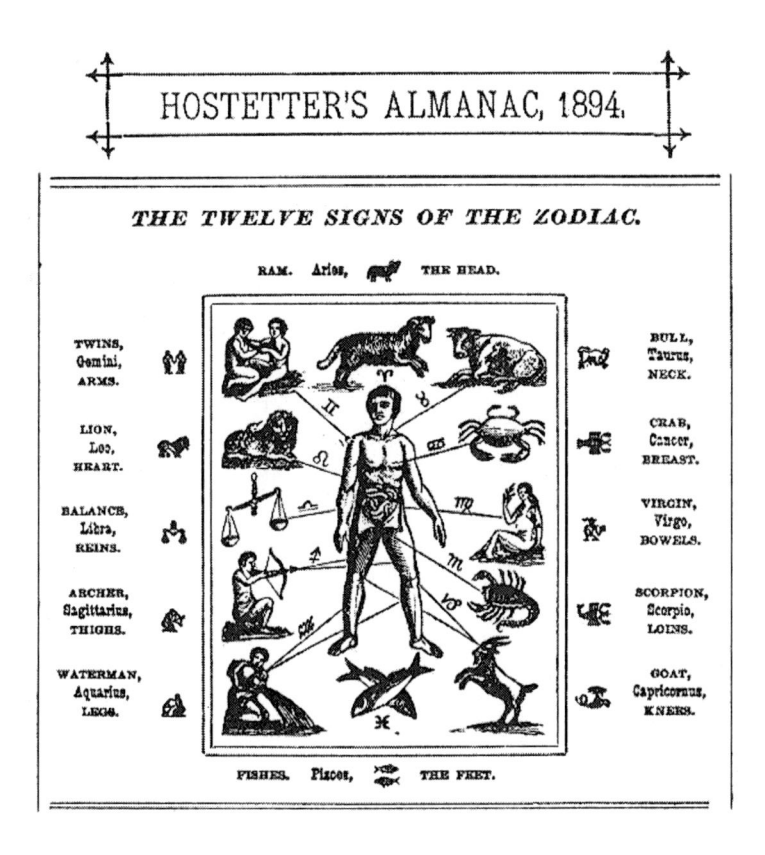

HOSTETTER'S ALMANAC, 1894.

THE TWELVE SIGNS OF THE ZODIAC.

RAM. Aries, THE HEAD.

TWINS, Gemini, ARMS.

BULL, Taurus, NECK.

LION, Leo, HEART.

CRAB, Cancer, BREAST.

BALANCE, Libra, REINS.

VIRGIN, Virgo, BOWELS.

ARCHER, Sagittarius, THIGHS.

SCORPION, Scorpio, LOINS.

WATERMAN, Aquarius, LEGS.

GOAT, Capricornus, KNEES.

FISHES. Pisces, THE FEET.

In the rite here the cube of space from the *Sefer Yetzirah* is used to orient the participants in a 3D space visualization. Each person standing in the circle visualizes each of the signs and tries to make contact with the sign and *'draw its energy down'*.

- ⊕ March 21st - April 20th Aries ♈
- ⊕ April 21st - May 21st Taurus ♉
- ⊕ May 22nd - June 21st Gemini ♊
- ⊕ June 22nd - July 22nd Cancer ♋
- ⊕ July 23rd - August 23rd Leo ♌
- ⊕ August 24th - September 23rd Virgo ♍
- ⊕ September 24th - October 23rd Libra ♎

- ⊕ October 24th - November 22nd Scorpio ♏
- ⊕ November 23rd - December 21st Sagittarius ♐
- ⊕ December 22nd - January 20th Capricorn ♑
- ⊕ January 21st - February 19th Aquarius ♒
- ⊕ February 20th - March 20th Pisces ♓

The assignment of which Zodiac sign to each edge shown here is following the Carlo Suares schema[4] rather than the Golden Dawn[6] schema. Carlo Suares schema works well for visualisations as set in the rite here, while Golden Dawn version allows linking to Tarot cosmology which is out of the scope of this work.

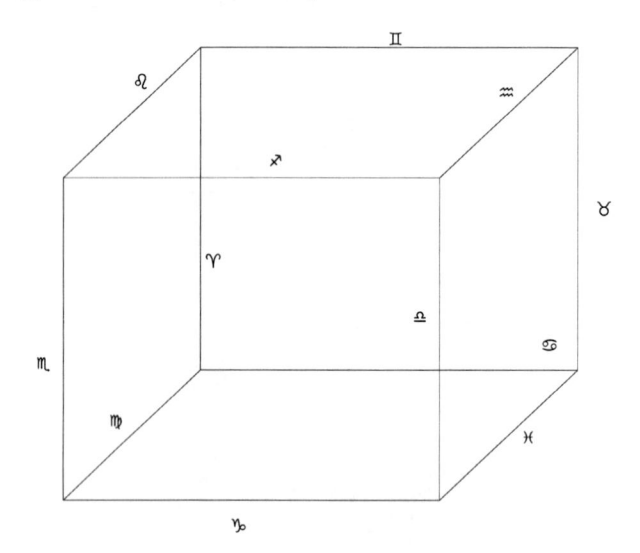

The focus of the rite is on the Zodiac; however it is also worth noticing the planetary directions on the cube of space as below. The planet Venus is in the north, Mercury in the south, Sun in the west and Mars in the east.[3,4,5,6]

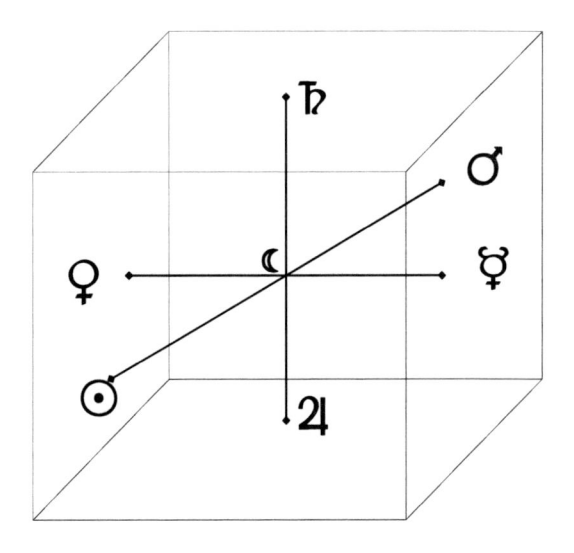

A Rite to the Zodiac

This rite is set up as a group ritual for thirteen people. Twelve participants each represent a sign of Zodiac and the 13th person is the journey person or the neophyte. The twelve should carry symbols representing the sign and should stand in the circle in the order of the Zodiac. The neophyte is one who is seeking to learn stellar lore. He/she waits in the antechamber (outside of the circle) until invited. Each of the signs has specific roles and lines to speak, in addition to the written lines they can add and say their own insights into constellations, it is encouraged each sign to say more than the stated lines. All should familiarise themselves with arrangement of Cube of Space and it should be discussed before the rite.

HIEROGLYPHIC PLAN BY HERMES, OF THE ANCIENT ZODIAC, FROM KIRCHER'S *OEDIPUS AEGYPTIACUS*, AS SHOWN IN *THE SECRET TEACHINGS OF ALL AGES* BY MANLY P HALL.[7]

The standard opening mentioned in the chapter *'opening and closing of rites'* is used here. This is then followed by:

Libra (walks to the neophyte and brings them from the antechamber): *Do you seek to learn of the mysteries of the Zodiac?*

Neophyte: Yes, *I seek to hear the music of the spheres.*

Leo: *The Chaldean Oracles of Zoroaster tells us the following of the heavens*

> "117. He maketh the whole World of Fire, Air, Water, and Earth, and of the all-nourishing Ether.
> 118. Placing Earth in the middle, but Water below the Earth, and Air above both these.
> 119. He fixed a vast multitude of un-wandering Stars, not by a strain laborious and hurtful, but with stability void of movement, forcing Fire forward into Fire.
> 120. The Father congregated the Seven Firmaments of the Cosmos, circumscribing the Heavens with convex form.

121. He constituted a Septenary of wandering Existences (the Planetary globes).
122. Suspending their disorder in Well-disposed Zones.
123. He made them six in number, and for the Seventh He cast into the midst thereof the Fiery Sun.
124. The Centre from which all (lines) which way soever are equal.
125. And that the Swift Sun doth pass as ever around a Centre.
126. Eagerly urging itself towards that Centre of resounding Light.
127. The Vast Sun, and the Brilliant Moon.
128. As rays of Light his locks flow forth, ending in acute points.
129. And of the Solar Circles, and of the Lunar, clashings, and of the Aerial Recesses; the Melody of Ether, and of the Sun, and of the phases of the Moon, and of the Air.
130. The most mystic of discourses informs us that His wholeness is in the Supra-mundane Orders for there a Solar World and Boundless Light subsist, as, the Oracles of the Chaldeans affirm.
131. The Sun more true measureth all things by time, being itself the time of time, according to the Oracle of the Gods concerning it.
132. The Disk (of the Sun) is borne in the Starless realm above the Inerratic Sphere; and hence he is, not in the midst of the Planets, but of the Three Worlds, according to the telestic Hypothesis.
133. The Sun is a Fire, the Channel of Fire, and the dispenser of Fire.
134. Hence Cronos, The Sun as Assessor beholds the true pole.
135. The Ethereal Course, and the vast motion of the Moon, and the Aerial fluxes.
136. O Ether, Sun, and Spirit of the Moon, ye are the chiefs of the Air.
137. And the wide Air, and the Lunar Course, and the Pole of the Sun.
138. For the Goddess bringeth forth the Vast Sun, and the lucent Moon.
139. She collecteth it, receiving the Melody of Ether, and of the Sun, and of the Moon, and of whatsoever things are contained in the Air.
140. Unwearied Nature ruleth over the Worlds and works, that the Heavens drawing downward might run an eternal course, and that the other periods of the Sun, Moon, Seasons, Night and Day, might be accomplished.
141. And above the shoulders of that Great Goddess, is Nature in her vastness exalted.
142. The most celebrated of the Babylonians, together with Ostanes and Zoroaster, very properly call the starry Spheres "Herds"; whether because these alone among corporeal magnitudes, are perfectly carried about around a Centre, or in conformity to the Oracles, because they are considered by them

as in a certain respect the bands and collectors of physical reasons, which they likewise call in their sacred discourse "Herds" (agelous) and by the insertion of a gamma (aggelous) Angels. Wherefore the Stars which preside over each of these herds are considered to be Deities or Dæmons, similar to the Angels, and are called Archangels; and they are seven in number.

143. Zoroaster calls the congruities of material forms to the ideals of the Soul of the World--Divine Allurements."[8]

All: to visualize the Cube of Space.

The neophyte walks toward Aries ask for its tale.

Aries: *I am the first sign of the zodiac, and once heralded the Spring Equinox. Even though an immortal Ram, I was given by goddess Nephele (cloud) to her children Phrixus and Helle to help them escape a sacrificial altar. To escape Hera I carried them from Europe to Asia. While flying over a narrow strait, Helle lost her grip on my Golden Fleece and feel into the strait, now called after her Hellespont. Poseidon rescued her and fathered a son by her called Paeon. I safely carried Phrixus to Colchis where he sacrificed me to Zeus and king of Colchis hung my golden fleece in his grove protected by a dragon until Jason and the Argonauts came and took it.*

In Egypt I am Ammon and my temple in Thebes still stands and has withstood the sands of time.[9,10,11,12,13]

Neophyte says thanks to Aries and walks to Taurus and asks for its tale.

Taurus: *I carried Europa the daughter of king of Sidon to Crete and Zeus as a reward placed me among the stars. He also took my shape to seduce her and she gave birth to Minos whose labyrinth house the Minotaur. In my stellar body Hyades and Pleiades the seven sisters are seen and my red eye is royal star Aldebaran.*

I was the first Age, and was slain by Mithras so there would be life and the next Age, the Age of Aries. [9,10,11,12,13]

Neophyte says thanks to Taurus and walks to Gemini and asks for its tale.

Gemini: *We are the twins Castor and Pollux the Dioscurides our mother was Leda and our father Zeus in his swan form. We were brothers of Helen of Troy and travelled with Jason and the Argonauts. We are the dual aspect of sky day and night, as after Castor died Zeus our father shared Pollux's immortality with both of us. Hence we* *spend alternate days in Olympus and Hades. We are saviour of sailors from shipwreck and St. Elmo's fire is our gift to them.*[9,10,11,12,13]

Neophyte says thanks to Gemini and walks to Cancer and asks for its tale.

Cancer: *I am the point of genesis the gates where souls descend from heavens to earthly bodies. Hera placed me among the stars for my loyalty to her by attacking Heracles who crushed me under his heel during our battle.*

Some of the stars of my body are called Asses (Asini) and were placed there by Dionysus. Dionysus, Hephaestus and the Satyrs rode Asses to battle the Giants, as a reward for our braying at the Giants and scaring them, we were placed in the heavens.

In Egypt I am the sacred scarab (dung beetle) and became Kheperi, god of the rising sun.[9,10,11,12,13]

Neophyte says thanks to Cancer and walks to Leo and asks for its tale.

Leo: *I fell from the sky as a shooting star and was raised by Hera and lived in Nemea, until when fighting Heracles he strangled me by his bare hands. He thereafter wore my lion skin; I am king of the beasts. I am the heat of the summer and royal star Regulus is part of me and my heart, and once summer solstice was in my sign.*[9,10,11,12,13]

Neophyte says thanks to Leo and walks to Virgo and asks for its tale.

Virgo: *I am the winged Maiden, I am Dike (Justice) the daughter of Zeus and Themis (Divine Law). I am also called Astraea, Isis and Demeter and I hold the star Spica the ear of wheat in my hand.*

As an immortal I lived and walked among humans in their Golden Age, and taught them and their tribal elders the laws. In this age humans lived like the gods without war, bloodshed and grief. After the Golden Age humans began to forget the laws and broke them. This led to the Silver Age and I visited humans less. When the Bronze Age and then Iron Age people came and started wars and eating meat and beef, I left the earth and flew to heaven where I stand with my sword and scale of justice.[9,10,11,12,13]

As Persephone you can see me in the sky from March till August so fields can grow, and then I descend to the underworld to be with my lover Hades. I am Ishtar too searching for my husband Tammuz in the underworld.

Neophyte says thanks to Virgo and walks to Libra and asks for its tale.

Libra: *I am the scales of justice that Virgo, Astraea or Dike holds. I am the balanced energy, the synthesis of matter and spirit. I am the equilibrium of day and of night. Once I used to rise at the Autumn Equinox, when the light and dark are equal, and life is held in balance on a knife edge. I am a breath held for a moment before breathing out. In Babylon I was all seeing Shamash's star of justice. I am the cosmic justice and the astral scale.*[9,10,11,12,13]

Neophyte says thanks to Libra and walks to Scorpio and asks for its tale.

Scorpio: *I am the slayer of Orion, when I rise in the night sky, Orion escapes and sets in the night sky. When Orion rises summer comes and I set and rains arrive. He boasted he could slay any creature that came from the earth, so Gaia sent me to kill him. I am dark, death and passion. The star of spirit the royal star Antares is my heart shining brightly red like Mars. I am at the southern extremities of the Milky Way.*[9,10,11,12,13]

Neophyte says thanks to Scorpio and walks to Sagittarius and asks for its tale.

Sagittarius: *I am the cosmic archer who is aiming my bow at the heart of Scorpio, the star Antares, I avenged Orion. I am also a bull slayer, when I rise Taurus sets. I am Crotus the son of Pan and Eupheme the nurse maid of Muses, and whom I lived with. Some see me as the immortal centaur Chrion the son of Cronus and Philrya. I am the union of material world (horse body), the soul (human bust), and the spirit (arrow). I advise sailors not sail when the sun is in my sign.*
[9,10,11,12,13]

Neophyte says thanks to Sagittarius and walks to Capricorn and asks for its tale.

Capricorn: *I am the point of apogenesis, the gates where souls ascend from earth to heavens, allowing the spirits released from earthly reincarnations to return to the stars. My helical rising was once at the winter solstice and sun's rebirth. I am the Aegipan that is the Goat Pan and I saved Jupiter from the Typhon by playing my pipe.*[9,10,11,12,13]

Neophyte says thanks to Capricorn and walks to Aquarius and asks for its tale.

Aquarius: *I am the water pourer, source of the cosmic waters and the astral sea which I pour from my jug. The royal star Fomalhaut is where the water from jug falls on. I am Ganymede the cup bearer to Zeus, and pour him the drink of the gods. When I appear in the night sky the rainy season starts. Welcome to my Age.* [9,10,11,12,13]

Neophyte says thanks to Aquarius and walks Pisces to and asks for its tale.

Pisces: *We are Venus and Cupid who to escape Typhon transformed ourselves to the two cosmic fishes, and escaped. We are connected by a cord and rise in the sky at the end of sun's yearly journey. My Age is coming to an end.* [9,10,11,12,13]

Neophyte says thanks to Pisces and walks to Aries completing the cycle.

Aries: *We the Zodiac are paired into gods and goddess:*[14]

Aries: Minerva	Libra: Vulcan
Taurus: Venus	Scorpio: Mars
Gemini: Apollo	Sagittarius: Diana
Cancer: Mercury	Capricorn: Vesta
Leo: Jupiter	Aquarius: Juno
Virgo: Ceres	Pisces: Neptune

All sit down to meditate for a while on what has been said, a relevant music could be played to help with the meditation and visualization of the Cube of Space and the nature of the interaction between the twelve constellations.

⊕ Saying of thanks to spirits of the place.
⊕ Final thanks to the Zodiac.

The standard closing mentioned in the chapter *'opening and closing of rites'* is used here. This is followed by having something to eat and drink. Clear the space.

References

1. *The Astrological Memory Theatre*, A T Mann, http://www.atmann.net/AstroMem1.htm
2. *The Lion and Unicorn Testify of Christ Part I: The Cornerstone Constellations*, by John P. Pratt, in *Meridian* Magazine (Nov. 8, 2001).
3. *Sefer Yetzirah/The Book of Creation: In Theory and Practice*, Aryeh Kaplan, (Red Wheel/Weiser, 1990).

4. *The Sefer Yetzirah: Cube of Space The Dimensions of Consciousness* by Carlo Suares.
 http://www.psyche.com/psyche/cube/cube.html & *The Sepher Yetsira,* Suares Carlo, Shambhala Publications, 1976.
5. *The Cube of Space* Archive Press & Communications, Kevin Townley, 1st edition, 1993.
6. *New Dimensions for the Cube of Space,* David Allen Hulse, Weiser Books, October 2000.
7. *The Secret Teachings of All Ages* by Manly P Hall, 1928.
8. *The Chaldean Oracles Attributed to Zoroaster,* Westcott, W.W, 1895.
9. *Astrology, Magic, and Alchemy in Art* by Matilde Battistini, Getty Trust Publications, 2007.
10. *Star Myths of the Greeks and Romans: A Sourcebook* by Theony Condos, Phanes Press, U.S. 1997.
11. *Sun, Moon & Stars* by Sheena McGrath, Capall Bann, 2005
12. *The Zodiac Experience,* by Patricia Crowther, Red Wheel/Weiser, 1992.
13. *The New Patterns in the Sky,* by Julius D.W. Staal, McDonald & Woodward Publishing Company, 1988.
14. Roman astrologer Marcus Manilius schema from: *A History of Western Astrology* by Jim Tester, Boydell Press, 1996.

Further reading:
Kabbalistic Astrology: The Sacred Tradition of the Hebrew Sages, Rabbi Joel C. Dobin, Inner Traditions,1999.
Sefer Yetzirah/The Book of Creation: In Theory and Practice, Aryeh Kaplan, Red Wheel/Weiser, 1990
The Sefer Yetzirah: Cube of Space The Dimensions of Consciousness, by Carlo Suares.
http://www.psyche.com/psyche/cube/cube.html & The Sepher Yetsira, Suares Carlo, Shambhala Publications, 1976.
The Cube of Space, Archive Press & Communications, Kevin Townley, 1st edition June 1993.
New Dimensions for the Cube of Space, David Allen Hulse, Weiser Books, October 2000.

Notes:

AURORA

(STONEHENGE, A MAGNIFICENT SITE WITH SOLAR ALIGNMENTS TO WATCH THE DAWN, PHOTO BY P. NABARZ).

INTRODUCTION

*"We three kings of Orient are
Bearing gifts we traverse afar
Field and fountain, moor and mountain
Following yonder star*

*O Star of wonder, star of night
Star with royal beauty bright
Westward leading, still proceeding
Guide us to thy Perfect Light....
-Carol We three Kings of Orient"*
- Rev. John Henry Hopkins (1857)

The Roman goddess of the dawn was called Aurora. This forms the last of our nocturnal rites, and we watch the golden dawn, the winged sun disc of Horus emerging from the horizon. We have journeyed across space in the body of Nuit or on Mithras' cloak; making contact with the distant stars and now with excitement we watch the sun rise, and making contact with our nearest star: the sun. The new dawn brings a new day and new possibilities; the rays of the sun awaken the land and hide the stars under its golden cloak and saffron robe, while her rosy figure opens the doors of the new day. The focus of this final rite in the series is the Roman Aurora or Greek Eos, however a brief mention from other systems is prudent.

In Thelema in *Liber Resh* we read facing East:

> "Hail unto Thee who art Ra in Thy rising, even unto Thee who art Ra in Thy strength, who travellest over the Heavens in Thy bark at the Uprising of the Sun. Tahuti standeth in His splendour at the prow, and Ra-Hoor abideth at the helm. Hail unto Thee from the Abodes of Night![1]"

In Zoroastrianism, Mithra is the protector of light of the dawn (*Havangah*), in Hinduism, Gayatri Mantra for the sun can be recited at dawn, to the great goddess of the dawn. In Yoga performing the '*Surya Namaskar*' or the salute to the sun at dawn can focus the mind and prepare one for the day ahead.

The story of Roman Aurora according to Thomas Bulfinch is as follows:

> "The goddess of the Dawn, like her sister the Moon, was at times inspired with the love of mortals. Her greatest favourite was Tithonus son of Laomedon, king of Troy. She stole him away, and prevailed on Jupiter to grant him immortality; but, forgetting to have youth joined in the gift, after some time she began to discern, to her great mortification, that he was growing old. When his hair was quite white she left his society; but he still had the range of her palace, lived on ambrosial food, and was clad in celestial raiment. At length he lost the power of using his limbs, and then she shut him up in his chamber, whence his feeble voice might at times be heard. Finally she turned him into a grasshopper.
>
> Memnon was the son of Aurora and Tithonus. He was king of the Ethiopians, and dwelt in the extreme east, on the shore of Ocean. He came with his warriors to assist the kindred of his father in the war of Troy. King Priam received him with great honours, and listened with admiration to his narrative of the wonders of the ocean shore.
>
> The very day after his arrival, Memnon, impatient of repose, led his troops to the field. Antilochus, the brave son of Nestor, fell by his hand, and the Greeks were put to flight, when Achilles appeared and restored the battle. A long and doubtful contest ensued between him and the son of Aurora; at length victory declared for Achilles, Memnon fell, and the Trojans fled in dismay.
>
> Aurora, who from her station in the sky had viewed with apprehension the danger of her son, when she saw him fall, directed his brothers, the Winds, to convey his body to the banks of the river Esepus in Paphlagonia. In the evening Aurora came, accompanied by the Hours and the Pleiades, and wept

and lamented over her son. Night, in sympathy with her grief, spread the heaven with clouds; all nature mourned for the offspring of the Dawn. The Ethiopians raised his tomb on the banks of the stream in the grove of the Nymphs, and Jupiter caused the sparks and cinders of his funeral pile to be turned into birds, which, dividing into two flocks, fought over the pile till they fell into the flames. Every year at the anniversary of his death they return and celebrate his obsequies in like manner. Aurora remains inconsolable for the loss of her son. Her tears still flow, and may be seen at early morning in the form of dew-drops on the grass.

Unlike most of the marvels of ancient mythology, there still exist some memorials of this. On the banks of the river Nile, in Egypt, are two colossal statues, one of which is said to be the statue of Memnon. Ancient writers record that when the first rays of the rising sun fall upon this statue a sound is heard to issue from it, which they compare to the snapping of a harp-string. There is some doubt about the identification of the existing statue with the one described by the ancients, and the mysterious sounds are still more doubtful. Yet there are not wanting some modern testimonies to their being still audible. It has been suggested that sounds produced by confined air making its escape from crevices or caverns in the rocks may have given some ground for the story. Sir Gardner Wilkinson, a late traveller, of the highest authority, examined the statue itself, and discovered that it was hollow, and that in the lap of the statue is a stone, which on being struck emits a metallic sound, that might still be made use of to deceive a visitor who was predisposed to believe its powers."[2]

The meaning of the Faravahar or the Holy Guardian Angel

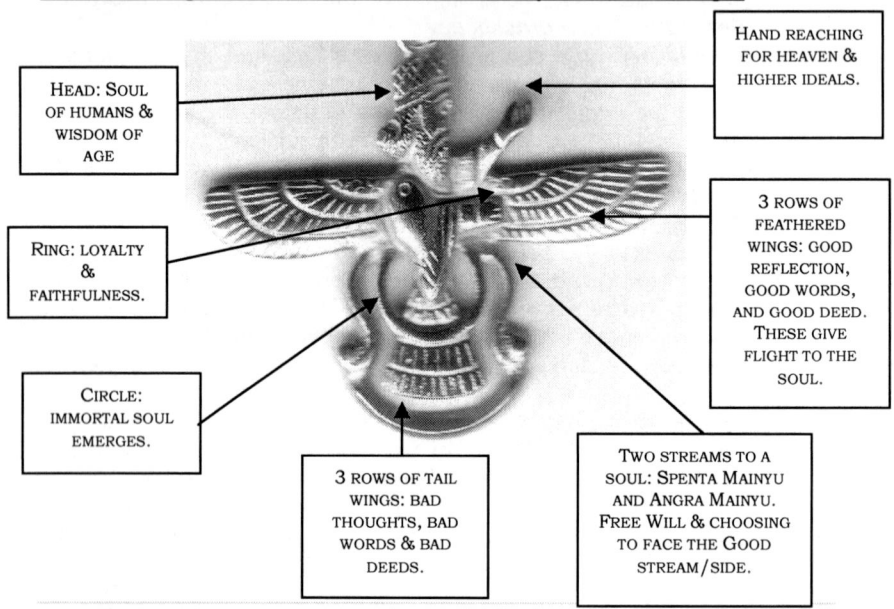

HEAD: SOUL OF HUMANS & WISDOM OF AGE

HAND REACHING FOR HEAVEN & HIGHER IDEALS.

RING: LOYALTY & FAITHFULNESS.

3 ROWS OF FEATHERED WINGS: GOOD REFLECTION, GOOD WORDS, AND GOOD DEED. THESE GIVE FLIGHT TO THE SOUL.

CIRCLE: IMMORTAL SOUL EMERGES.

3 ROWS OF TAIL WINGS: BAD THOUGHTS, BAD WORDS & BAD DEEDS.

TWO STREAMS TO A SOUL: SPENTA MAINYU AND ANGRA MAINYU. FREE WILL & CHOOSING TO FACE THE GOOD STREAM/SIDE.

Marking Dawn and sun rise from the East the Egyptian winged disk, the Herakhty (Horus of Horizon), is linked to the Assyrian winged disk, and the Persian *Faravahar* winged disc (Holy Guardian Angels). The Assyrian winged disk is Anshar which means *'Horizon of Heaven'* and like the Egyptian winged disk is male and solar. The Faravahar symbol in Zoroastrianism represents the Fravashi (the person's Guardian Angel/spirit) they come down from heaven to stand by each person from their birth and are prayed to for guidance and protection. They are called the Bountiful Immortals.

AURORA RITE

An altar to Dawn, Aurora: the edge of the sword represents the horizon; the seven candles (large red middle candle) represent dawn. The seven candles can also be seen as the Persian Faravahar or the Egyptian winged sun disc which represents the golden dawn, the sun and its light (photo by P. Nabarz).

Set up
- ⊕ Location: a place with good visibility of dawn.
- ⊕ Candles or tea lights to be lit and place on altar in a straight line to give impression of dawn coming over the horizon.
- ⊕ Central fire might be needed due to cold before dawn.
- ⊕ Time to perform this rite is at dawn
- ⊕ Clothing: sensible outdoor clothing & footwear.

- ⊕ Altar cloth to have stars on it.
- ⊕ Offerings.
- ⊕ Face paint or body paint e.g. Henna or Woad or commercial ones from party shops.
- ⊕ Food and drink to share.

Use the body paint (e.g. Henna) to draw image of dawn, semi circle with rays emerging.

The standard opening mentioned in the chapter *'opening and closing of rites'* is used here. This is then followed by:

Light the candles which are set in a straight line for dawn.

If you are familiar with the Yoga moves of *'Surya Namaskar'* or the salute to the sun, perform these before declaring your intent.

Declare your intent as wanting to connect to Aurora and to *'draw down'* the power of Aurora into yourself (if that is part of your intent).

While looking at the sky, next take relaxed the stance.

Mediate on Aurora while standing in this position for few minutes.

When you feel ready recite the following hymn to Aurora. Before you recite visualise a door in front of you which has the dawn painted on it and dawn emerges from it as it opens.

DAWN, PHOTO BY P. NABARZ

DAWN, PHOTO BY P. NABARZ

Orphic hymn to Aurora. LXXVII.
(The Fumigation from Manna)

>"Hear me, O Goddess! whose emerging ray
>Leads on the broad refulgence of the day;
>Blushing Aurora, whose celestial light
>Beams on the world with reddening splendours bright:
>Angel of Titan, whom with constant round,
>Thy orient beams recall from night profound:
>Labour of every kind to lead is thine,
>Of mortal life the minister divine.
>Mankind in thee eternally delight,
>And none presumes to shun thy beauteous sight.
>Soon as thy splendours break the bands of rest,
>And eyes unclose with pleasing sleep oppressed;
>Men, reptiles, birds, and beasts, with general voice,
>And all the nations of the deep, rejoice;
>For all the culture of our life is thine.
>Come, blessed power! and to these rites incline:
>Thy holy light increase, and unconfined
>Diffuse its radiance on thy mystic's mind."[3]

Sit down to meditate for a while on what has been said, relevant music could be played to help with the meditation.

⊕ Saying of thanks to spirits of the place.
⊕ Final thanks to Aurora.

The standard closing mentioned in the chapter *'opening and closing of rites'* is used here. This is followed by having something to eat and drink. Then clear the space.

References

1. *Liber Resh vel Helios sub figura CC* by Aleister Crowley.
2. *Bulfinch's mythology the age of fable or stories of gods and heroes* by Thomas Bulfinch,1855.
3. *The Hymns of Orpheus* translated by Thomas Taylor, 1792.

For further info on Faravahar see:
http://www.crystalinks.com/faravahar.html &
http://altreligion.about.com/od/symbols/a/faravahar.htm

Notes:

THE STELLAR WORLD CAVE

P. NABARZ IN WEST KENNET LONG BARROW, PHOTO BY ALISON JONES.

INTRODUCTION

"Mithras who under the rocks of the Persian Cave twists the horns of the stubborn Bull"
- Statius 80 AD

"Hail to you ladder of the god! Hail to you ladder of Seth! Stand up, ladder of the god! Stand up, ladder of Seth! Stand up, ladder of Horus, which was made for Osiris so that he might ascend on it to the sky and escort Ra...you ascend to the sky upon ladder of god..."[1] - The Ancient Egyptian Pyramid Texts.

"When you ascend to the sky, your power upon you, your terror about you, your magic at your feet, you are helped by Atum just as he used to do, the gods who are in the sky are brought to you, the gods who are on the earth assemble for you, they place their hands under you, they make a ladder for you that you may ascend on it to the sky, the doors of the sky are opened for you, the doors of the starry firmament are thrown open for you"[2] - The Ancient Egyptian Pyramid Texts.

The ancient Roman religion of the Mysteries of Mithras, due to its cosmology and practical approach, was immensely popular not only among the Legions, but also with merchants; crossing social class barriers. From the late first century BC until 400 AD it was taken to every corner of the Roman Empire. In the introductory chapter the concept of the Mithraeum as the World Cave was introduced. Now we come back full circle, like the Ouroboros. We have journeyed through a number of stars, constellations, the moon and the planets. We have seen the stellar relationships within the cube of space. All these come together in forming the World Cave as described in Porphyry; a cube of space as a sphere, which fits well with the view of the universe as a space that has been ever expanding since the big bang. The Cave is the microcosm, and the Magi inside it aim to connect to the World Soul, which is surrounded by the four Royal Stars or Stellar Guardians (Eagle, Bull, Man, Lion).

Unlike the previous chapters there are no hymns, poems or invocations; instead this rite consists of mainly a silent meditation and visualisation. You are now familiar with the myths, legends and current of the constellations. You are ready to venture into the World Cave, comfortably knowing all the signs and symbols and connect to the World Soul.

From a Neo-Platonic view the initiate's aim is to ascend and return to the Source, the constellation Cancer is the gate through which souls descend (genesis) and Capricorn the gate through which they ascend (apogenesis). The journey is made along the Milky Way; the river of souls or stars. The seven planets are the first stepping stones in this process and being liberated from their influence, the initiate passes through the eight gates into the realms and of the fixed stars and continues their Ascension until they reach their Star in the company of heaven. The Sci-Fi fans of Star Gate have been absorbing much magical lore via the medium of modern story telling; the journey through the star gate depends also on knowing the planetary and the constellation signs!

In the world view of apogenesis; this is what happens to everyone after they die, however, the initiates begin the process while still alive and *'die before they die'*, they learn the signs and actively make their journey to their Star. It is an interesting synchronicity that burials in cave like structures are part of many cultures, from Neolithic Long Barrows to Christian Crypts. The cave is an ancient allegory of the world. Porphyry in *'On the Cave of the Nymphs'* in the Thirteenth Book of the *Odyssey* tells us:

> "...*After this Zoroaster likewise, it was usual with others to perform the rites pertaining to the mysteries in caverns and*

dens, whether spontaneously produced, or made by the hands. For as they established temples, groves, and altars to the celestial Gods, but to the terrestrial Gods, and to heroes, altars alone, and to the subterranean divinities pits and cells; so to the world they dedicated caves and dens; as likewise to Nymphs, on account of the water which trickles, or is diffused in caverns, over which the Naiades, as we shall shortly observe, preside. Not only, however, did the ancients make a cavern, as we have said, to be a symbol of the world, or of a generated and sensible nature: but they also assumed it as a symbol of all invisible powers; because as caverns are obscure and dark, so the essence of these powers is occult. Hence Saturn fabricated a cavern in the ocean itself and concealed in it his children. Thus, too, Ceres educated Proserpine with her Nymphs in a cave; and many other particulars of this kind may be found in the writings of theologists. But that the ancients dedicated caverns to Nymphs and especially to Naiades, who dwell, near fountains, and who are called Naiades from the streams over which they preside, is manifest from the hymn to Apollo, in which it is said: " The Nymphs residing in caves shall deduce fountains of intellectual waters to thee (according to the divine voice of the Muses), which are the progeny of a terrene spirit. Hence waters, bursting through every river, shall exhibit to mankind perpetual effusions of sweet streams". From hence, as it appears to me the Pythagoreans and after them Plato, showed that the world is a cavern and a den. For the powers which are the leaders of souls, thus speak in a verse of Empedocles: "Now at this secret cavern we're arrived." Also by Plato, in the seventh book of his Republic, it is said, Behold men as if dwelling in a subterraneous cavern, and in a denlike habitation, whose entrance is widely expanded to the admission of the light through the whole cave." But when the other person in the dialogue says: You adduce an unusual and wonderful similitude," he replies, "The whole of this image, friend Glauco, must be adapted to what has been before said, assimilating this receptacle, which is visible through the sight to the habitation of a prison; but the light of the fire which is in it to the power of the sun. That theologists, therefore, considered caverns as symbols of the world, and of mundane powers, is through this, manifest. And it has been already observed by us, that they also considered a cave as a symbol of the intelligible essence; being impelled to do so by different and not the same conceptions. For they were of opinion that a cave is a symbol of the sensible world because caverns are dark, stony, and humid; and they asserted that the world is a thing of this kind, through the matter of which it consists, and through its repercussive and flowing nature. But they thought it to be a symbol of the intelligible world, because that world is invisible to sensible perception, and possesses a firm and stable essence ..."[3]

The following rite and meditation on the World Cave combines what has been absorbed in working with the stellar material in this book. We enter the ancient's Planetarium.

In a sense the entire book is a prelude to this meditation. The meditation takes us to become an active part and component of the World Axis and to become aware and connected to the World Soul. The meditation completes with sight of the World Axis (*Axis Mundi*) as a sight that many Magi, Shamans, and Magical practitioners from different cultures have seen through the ages. We see that the Christian, Golden Dawn and Kabbalistic views of the Throne of Heaven, the Nordic Yggdrasil the world Ash tree, the Greek Omphalos, the Tower of Babel, the Voodoo *poteau-mitan,* and the Spindle of Necessity, Shiva lingam etc ... all are linked and are human interpretations of the same *'thing'* that exists in other worlds, in the astral and stellar realms. This is a thread of infinity that pierces each world at the pole star - the keystone, and Sufi's *Qutub*.

One can climb the World Tree to other worlds, or hang like Odin from the Ash tree, or become part of the Throne of Heaven by sitting in a chair which is the Throne, or, like Heracles and Perseus take the Golden Apples from the Garden of the Hesperides (located at the Little Bear/Pole Star guarded by constellation Draco), fly around the *Stambha*, the Shiva Lingam, dance circling the *poteau-mitan,* stand at the top of a Ziggurat, receive feathers from the bird Simurgh who sits on the top of mount Qaf (*axis mundi*): all are reflections of the same *'thing'*. This is where the Shamans and Magicians interaction differs from Orthodox religion's clergy; for example, in the *Book of Revelation* the Throne of Heaven is to be worshipped and the Apostle Paul's interaction is one of observation and worship only. In another Christian observation, it is Lucifer who wanted the Throne of Heaven and this caused his fall. Jacob, Paul and many others who have ascended to this point are simply worshiping the Throne, or want to take it; both approaches fail. In The Myth of *Er* we again see a description of the Throne this time as Spindle of Necessity. In the *Dream of Scipio* another vision of the Throne is described. The Mystic's and Magician's interaction with the Throne or Axis Mundi as we see in the meditation below is quite different.

Rite of the Stellar World Cave

The Crypt in Winchester Cathedral, photo by P.Nabarz

THE MITHRAEUM (BY TORIN GOLDING, ROMA) IN SECOND LIFE, SHOWN HERE AS A VISUAL AID.

The standard opening mentioned in the chapter *'opening and closing of rites'* is used here. This rite consists of two parts, A and B. Part A consists of the stellar cave mediation; part B is the journey beyond the cave. This rite can be carried out as a cave mediation and closed within the cave, or part B, which is suitable for more experienced practitioners may be incorporated. Part B cannot be performed alone as it follows on in sequence from Part A.

Part A (After the Opening Rite)

Cave meditation:

Visualise yourself standing in a front of a cave. The sun is beating down on you; it is a bright warm day.

In front of the cave stand two Roman Centurions, guarding the way. Walk up to them and great them by saying *Nama* (*Hail*) and ask to be admitted into the Mithraeum. Thank the guardians and enter. As you walk further in the cave, the day light behind you fades. Eventually you reach some steps in the cave, there are seven steps leading down to the bottom of the cave.

You can smell incense wafting out, walk down the seven steps, you are faced with the interior of the Mithraeum. You notice two statues are flanking you, like two great pillars, they are the two torchbearers, Cautes and Cautopates, symbolising the equinoxes. Cautes' torch is pointing upwards: the spring equinox and much light, warmth and heat emanates from it. Cautopates' torch is pointing downwards: the autumn equinox and less light and heat emanates from his torch. They wear red cloaks and red caps of liberty.

There are people sitting and meditating, some are chanting *Ya Doust Mithra*; the cave is lit by torches and candle light, you can smell the incense burning and hear the sound of water dripping from the moist cave walls, the stone under your feet feels cold and solid, you are aware that all the four elements are present in their multitude.

Looking ahead of you, you can see the symbols of seven planets drawn on the floor, with a gateway drawn between each. The symbols reach toward the end of the cave where an image of Mithras slaying the Bull is visible. As you step onto the first square, visualise a door with the symbol of Mercury on it. As you stand on the symbol of Mercury, reflect on what you learned about this planet when you performed the rite to the seven planets. When ready, visualise a door with the symbol of Venus, walk through the door onto the Venus symbol and reflect on what you have absorbed about this planet from the performing the rites of the seven planets. Next, visualise a door with the symbol of Mars, step onto the Mars symbol, and reflect on what you have learned about this planet. Next, visualise a door with the symbol of Jupiter, step onto the Jupiter symbol, and reflect on what you have learned about this planet. Next, visualise a door with the symbol of the Moon, step onto the Moon symbol and reflect on what you have learned about the moon when you draw down her power. Next, visualise a door with the symbol of the Sun, step onto the Sun symbol and reflect on the light you have absorbed from this star. Next, visualise a door with the symbol of Saturn, step onto the Saturn symbol and reflect on the time you have learned from this planet.

Now you stand towards end of the cave, at the eighth doorway, the realm of the fixed stars, facing scene of Mithras slaying the Bull. As you look at the walls of the cave you see the twelve signs of the Zodiac painted on the walls around you. Starting from your left, you see the signs of spring: Aries, Taurus, Gemini, then the signs of summer: Cancer, Leo and Virgo. As you continue turning you can see the signs of autumn painted on the wall: Libra, Scorpio, Sagittarius; then the signs of the winter: Capricorn, Aquarius, Pisces.

You stand in this cave, with the signs of the seven planets on the floor and the signs of the Zodiac on the walls. That is, you stand with planets below you as you have journeyed up from them and you are surrounded by the twelve constellations of the Zodiac; they are around you, and you stand among them as they circle the earth. Leo is in the south, Aquarius in the north, Taurus in the east and Scorpio in the west.

Now shift your gaze from the floor and walls to the ceiling of the cave, here you can see more stars and constellations painted. There are many constellations on the ceiling, the Great Bear (Plough), Draco, the Little Bear (and the Pole star), Cepheus, Cassiopeia, Perseus, Andromeda, Cygnus, Canis Major, Orion, the Pleiades and many others. Take your time as you reflect back on all you have absorbed and learned about these constellations and others as you worked your way through their rites. Allow yourself to flow with the knowledge you have of the constellations, let links between the stars be formed and patterns emerge.

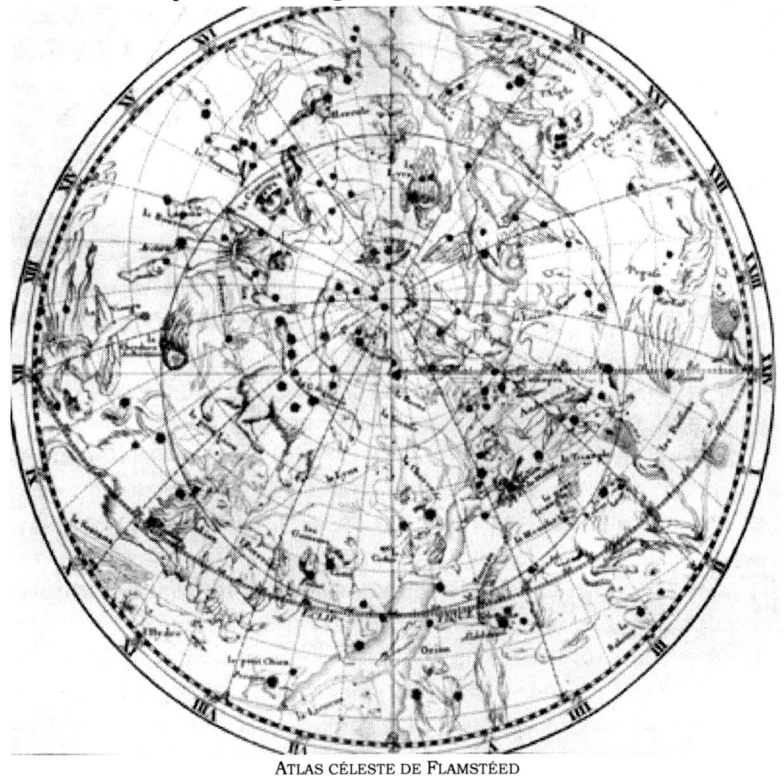

ATLAS CÉLESTE DE FLAMSTÉED

You stand with planets below you, the Zodiac around you and Great Bear, Draco, Cygnus many other constellations above you. You are standing in the centre of Cave, the Universe, the Microcosm of all that is.

Take your time to get used to all the connections; you may want to finish the meditation at this stage and return and perform the closing of the rite.

Part B

If you wish to journey further and are comfortable and experienced enough, then the stellar journey can be continued to realms beyond the stars.

Visualise the walls of the cave becoming transparent, and see the cave expand, the planets slowly disappear from below you, as you begin flying in space, upwards, the Zodiac around you also begins to fade as you head towards the pole star.

The stellar space transforms into a desert-like landscape, a vague path can be seen in the sand and you follow it. Eventually, you can see someone approaching, as you approach the person you recognise yourself walking towards you! A mirage perhaps? As you reach the other you, your higher self extends their right hand, and as you shake hands, you recognise your higher self, you blend into one, you are now complete.

The next step of the journey is for few. You continue to follow the path in the sand, with many suns in sky shining down. The path leads to a stone platform, three steps lead to the platform; this is a platform for the dead.

At end of the platform is a perfect stone cube (*Ashlar*); balanced on top of it is a ladder, with seven steps which leads into space. You may want to end the visualisation and return now.

If you wish to journey further and are comfortable and experienced enough, then begin climbing the ladder, as you reach the seventh step, it feels as if you have reached a ceiling, a resistance. If you are ready, then push against the resistance, this will give way to an opening, a hatch. As you force yourself through the hatch you are faced with nothingness, darkness, the void. The light from the hatch fades as you begin making your way across the abyss. Why are you here? What do you seek? To be one with Source? Union with a beloved God? To find your star? Knowledge? Why are you making this journey? To be one with source, the One, the Monad. Beginning of my Beginning, Origin of my Origins. To fully connect in every sense.

A heavenly throne or chair appears, pulled by a Lion, a Bull, an Eagle and a Man. Will you take the seat? Is this the throne in which the Morning Star wanted to sit, the throne which caused his fall? To be the fifth star at the height of heaven, surrounded by the four. No, only god should sit on the throne of heaven? Refuse the throne! Can you refuse it?

The journey ends here for some. You may want to end the visualisation and return now.

Those who refuse the throne are shown a wondrous sight, mist dissolves around the throne, and next to the throne is another identical throne or chair, and next to that one another chair and another chair. There are hundreds of identical thrones above and below, as well as on both sides of the throne you were offered. There are different people, sitting on them. They are those who made this journey before, the initiates who have reached this stage. They speak to you, and the mists dissolve further, all the thrones are part of a structure. The whole of the structure is the throne of heaven! You can see The Throne of heaven is made of thousands of individual thrones, with an initiate hierophant sitting in each. Your spiritual guides through your life appear next to you. The chair offered to you is only 'a' throne of heaven and not 'the' Throne of heaven. The throne of the initiate offered to you is for you, it has always been there, for you to return to it. As you finally take your seat, and go through the chair you become part of all the initiate hierophants on their thrones. You become aware of your connection to them; you are a branch on the tree, a brick in the wall night sky or the Throne Heaven. A part of whole, a drop in ocean, yet now you are one with the ocean. You wish to see more of The Throne of heaven? Your throne is your Chariot, which is drawn by the four Cherubim star constellations (a Lion, a Bull, an Eagle and a Man), and you fly around The Throne of heaven. You can see that The Throne of heaven expands into infinity, above and below, made of millions of thrones with millions of initiates sitting in them. The Throne is a Tower rotating clockwise, a Tower of infinity spanning all realities. This Throne was the inspiration of the Ziggurats, and the Tower of Babel, was aiming to connect to it. This is the *Stambha* and Shiva Lingam penetrating all worlds, connecting them. The Tower turns like a giant spindle, galaxies turning with it. Yggdrasil the world Ash tree, the Omphalos, the *poteau-mitan,* and the Spindle of Necessity, a thread that goes through the fabric of space at all the Pole Stars, the Sufi *Qutub*. The cosmic axis or world pillar: the *axis mundi* is this Tower of Heaven that rotates, spreading creation, light, life, love and liberty. In your chair, you blend with the Source, the first spark that created the Tower/Throne at its centre. You are also part of the World Soul, the *Anima mundi.* Time and space fade, you are a star in the company of heaven. You sit among all initiates through the ages from around the world who have observed the same sight with many different interpretations and have become part of it.

The journey ends for now, and you should return, reversing the whole journey, all the way back to the cave.

Saying of thanks to the Throne of Heaven, the initiates, spirits and guides you have meet.

Final thanks to Guardians of the cave.

The standard closing mentioned in the chapter *'opening and closing of rites'* is used here. This is followed by having something to eat and drink. Then clear the space.

You should spend a significant amount of time earthing yourself after this journey, as well as eating and drinking, try doing some gardening or spend time with friends and family or go for a gentle walk.

References:

1. Utterance 478, from line 971 invocation of the ladder to the sky, *The Ancient Egyptian Pyramid Texts*, by R. O. Faulkner, (Clarendon Press, 1969) p165-166.
2. Utterance 572, lines 1472-1475 an ascension text, *The Ancient Egyptian Pyramid Texts*, by R. O. Faulkner, (Clarendon Press, 1969) p227.
3. Porphyry in *'On the Cave of the Nymphs'*, Translated by Thomas Taylor, 1917.

Notes:

EPILOGUE: MONAD

Monad
(A Winter Solstice inspired poem).

"Calling on a dream, a fleeting feeling,
a longing, a gaping hole, on origin of origins;
the golden spiral to the beginning to the Monad.

Sword in one hand, and a pen in the other.
Maat weighing your heart;
sword into the stone, pen to the paper.

The Raven and the Dove circling over head,
bringing a skull and an olive branch,
braid the olive leaves into the skull;
Peace in death.

Die before you die.
Morrigan's lover, ash on the forehead, widow's son,
wrapped in a white shroud; Lugh slain and risen.
The long winter night, battered by the waves of memory.
The Bard will remember, Birch, new leaf.

A river of life filled with pebbles of death,
so many pebbles, to dam the flow.
white collars, black turbans, grey suits; Satan get behind me;
the Prince of lies, offering his One True Way.

The river keeps on flowing;
in time under the mill of love, rough Ashlar becomes smooth,
pebbles become sparkling gems and stepping stones.
Aeon and Maat hand in hand, beyond the fixed stars.
Whispering every man and woman is a star."

-Nabarz (15 December 2008)

Ya Hu

BIBLIOGRAPHY

AND FURTHER READING:

Abusch, Tzvi; *Ascent to the Stars in a Mesopotamian Ritual*; 1995; in *Death, Ecstasy, and Other Worldly Journeys*; p18-23; Collins, John J. & Fishbane, Michael (eds); State University of New York Press; Albany.

Allan, Tony; *Wise Lord of the Sky: Persian Myth*; 1999; Time Life Books.

Apuleius, Lucius "Africanus", & Adlington, William (trans); *The Golden Ass*; 1566, sacred-texts.com.

Atallah, Hashem (trans) & Kiesel, William (ed); *Picatrix Ghayat al Hakim or The Goal of the Wise;* 2002; Ouroboros Press; Seattle.

Bakhtiar, Laleh; *Sufi Expressions of the Mystic Quest; 1997;* Thames and Hudson; London.

Bardon, Franz; *Initiation into Hermetics;* 2001; Merkur Publishing; Utah.

Barrett, Francis; *The Magus: Or Celestial Intelligencer;* 2007; Nonsuch publishing Ltd.

Battistini, Matilde; *Astrology, Magic, and Alchemy in Art;* 2007; Getty Trust Publications; Los Angeles.

Bauval, Robert, & Gilbert, Adrian; *The Orion Mystery: Unlocking the Secrets of the Pyramids*; 1995; Mandarin; Hawaii.

Bauval, Robert, & Hancock, Graham; *Keeper of Genesis: A Quest for the Hidden Legacy of Mankind*; 1996; William Heinemann Ltd; London.

Beck, Roger; *A Brief History of Ancient Astrology (Brief Histories of the Ancient World)*; 2006; Blackwell Publishing; Oxford.

Beck, Roger; *The Religion of the Mithras Cult in the Roman Empire: Mysteries of the Unconquered Sun*; 2006; Oxford University Press; Oxford.

Betz, Hans Dieter (ed); *The Greek Magical Papyri in Translation: Including the Demotic Spells: Texts*; 1997; University Of Chicago Press; Chicago.

Betz, Hans Dieter; *Mithras Liturgy: Text, Translation, & Commentary*; *Studies & Texts in Antiquity & Christianity, 18*; 2003; Paul Mohr Verlag.

Boroff, Marie; *Stars and Other Signs*; 2003; Yale University Press; Yale.

Boyce, Mary; *Textual sources for the study of Zoroastrianism;* 1990; University of Chicago Press; Chicago.

Buchanan-Brown, John & Chevalier, Jean & Gheerbrant, Alain; *The Penguin Dictionary of Symbols*; 1996; Penguin Books Ltd; London.

Budge, E. A. Wallis; *Legends of the Gods: The Egyptian Texts, edited with Translations*; 1912; Kegan Paul; London.

Bulfinch, Thomas; *Bulfinch's Mythology The Age of Fable or Stories of Gods and Heroes*; 1855; sacred-texts.com and gutenberg.org

Burckhardt, Titus; *Mystical Astrology According to Ibn Arabi*; 1977; Beshara Publications; Cheltenham.

Callimachus, & Lycophron, & Aratus, & Mair, A.W. (trans), & Mair, G.R. (trans); *Callimachus: Hymns and Epigrams, Lycophron and Aratus*; 1921; Loeb Classical Library No. 129; Harvard.

Chishti, Shaykh Hakim Moinuddin; *The Book of Sufi Healing*; 1991; Inner Traditions; Vermont.

Churton, Tobias; *The Magus of Freemasonry: The Mysterious Life of Elias Ashmole - Scientist, Alchemist and Founder of the Royal Society*; 2006; Inner Traditions; Vermont.

Cicero, &. Peabody, Andrew P. (trans, ed); *Scipio's Dream*, http://ancienthistory.about.com/library/bl/bl_text_cic_scipiodream.htm

Clark, Peter; *Zoroastrianism: An Introduction to an Ancient Faith*; 1998; Sussex Academic Press; Sussex.

Clouter, Gregory; *The Lost Zodiac of the Druids*; 2003; Vega; London.

Collins, Andrew; *The Cygnus Mystery: Unlocking the Ancient Secret of Life's Origins in the Cosmos*; 2006; Watkins Publishing; London.

Condos, Theony; *Star Myths of the Greeks and Romans: A Sourcebook*; 1997; Phanes Press; Michigan.

Conway, David; *Complete Magic Primer*, 1988; Thorsons; Wellingborough.

Copenhaver, Brian P.; *Hermetica: The Greek "Corpus Hermeticum" and the Latin "Asclepius" in a New English Translation*; 1995; Cambridge University Press; Cambridge.

Coppens, Philip; *The Canopus Revelation: The Stargate of the Gods and the Ark of Osiris*; 2004; Adventures Unlimited Press; Illinois.

Corbin, Henry; *Creative Imagination in the Sufism of Ibn 'Arabi*; 1981; Princeton University Press; Princeton.

----------; *Spiritual Body and Celestial Earth: From Mazdean Iran to Shi'ite Itan*; 1990; Princeton University Press; Princeton.

----------; *The Man of Light in Iranian Sufism*; 1994; Omega Publications; New York.

Cotterell, Arthur; *The Ultimate Encyclopaedia of Mythology*; 2003; Hermes House; London.

Crowley, Aleister; *Magick in Theory and Practice*; 1994; Red Wheel Weiser; Maine.

----------; *Liber CVI, Liber XV 'The Gnostic Mass', Liber AL vel Legis, Liber LXV (Liber Cordis Cincti Serpente, The Book of the Heart Girt with a Serpent), Liber Resh vel Helios sub figura CC*, sacred-texts.com

Crowther, Patricia; *The Zodiac Experience: Initiation through the 12 Signs*; 1992; Red Wheel Weiser; Maine.

Cumont, Franz; *Astrology and Religion Among the Greeks and Romans*; 1912; sacred-texts.com.

Darmesteter, James (trans); *Avesta: Khorda Avesta, Book of Common Prayer*, from *Sacred Books of the East*; 1898; sacred-texts.com and avesta.org

---------- (trans); *Yasht 19, 50. The Zend Avesta*, Part II (SBE23); 1882, sacred-texts.com

Davies, Dick; *Epic and Sedition: The Case of Ferdowsi's Shahnameh*; 2006; Mage Publishers; Washington DC.

Dobin, Rabbi Joel C.; *Kabbalistic Astrology: The Sacred Tradition of the Hebrew Sages*; 1999; Inner Traditions; Vermont.

Drake, Joseph Rodman; *The Culprit Fay*; 1836; George Dearborn; New York

Eason, Cassandra; *A Complete Guide to Night Magic*; 2002; Piatkus Books; London.

Faulkner, R.O.; *The Ancient Egyptian Pyramid Texts*; 1969; Clarendon Press; Oxford

Feild, Reshad; *The Last Barrier a Sufi journey*; 1990; Element Books; Salisbury.

Ferdowsi, Abolqasem, & Zimmern, Helen (trans); *Shah Nameh The Epic of Kings*; 1883; sacred-texts.com.

Ferdowsi, Abolqasem, & Davies, Dick (trans); *Shah Nameh The Persian book of Kings*; 2007; Penguin Classics; London.

Flowers, Stephen Edred; *Hermetic Magic: The Postmodern Magickal Papyrus of Abaris*; 1995; Red Wheel Weiser; Maine.

Fries, Jan; *Seidways: Shaking, Swaying and Serpent Mysteries*; 1996; Mandrake of Oxford; Oxford.

-----------; *Helrunar: A Manual of Rune Magick*; 2002; Mandrake of Oxford; Oxford.

Frye, Richard N.; *The Heritage of Persia*; 1993; Mazda Publishers; California.

-----------; *Ibn Fadlans' journey to Russia: a tenth-century traveller from Baghdad*; 2006; Markus Wiener; Princeton.

Gardner, Gerald; *The Gardnerian Book of Shadows*; sacred-texts.com

Gershevitch, Ilya (trans); *The Avestan Hymn to Mithra*; 2008; Cambridge University Press; Cambridge.

Gilbert, Adrian; *Signs in the Sky: Astrological and Archaeological Evidence That We Are Entering a New Age*; 2005; ARE Press; Virginia.

-----------; *Magi: The Quest for the Secret Tradition*; 1996; Bloomsbury Publishing PLC; London.

Grant, Kenneth; *Outer Gateways*; 1994; Skoob Esoterica; London.

-----------; *Outside the Circles of Time*; 2008; Starfire Publishing Ltd; London.

Guest, Lady Charlotte; *The Mabinogion*; 1877; sacred-texts.com

Hall, Manly P.; *The Secret Teachings of All Ages*; 1928; sacred-texts.com.

Hand Clow, Barbara; *The Pleiadian Agenda: A New Cosmology for the Age of Light*; 1995; Bear & Company; Vermont.

Hara, Hashnu O.; *Practical Yoga and Persian Magic*; 2003; Kessinger Publishing Co; Montana.

Hawke, Elen; *Praise to the Moon: Magic and Myth of the Lunar Cycle*; 2002; Llewellyn Publications; Minnesota.

Hesiod, & Evelyn-White, H.G. (trans); *Works And Days*; 1914; sacred-texts.com

Hogart, R.C. (trans); *Hymns of Orpheus*; 1993; Phanes Press; Michigan.

Homer, & Evelyn-White, H.G. (trans); *The Homeric Hymns*; 1914, sacred-texts.com

Homer, & Butler, Samuel (trans); *Book V, The Odyssey*; 1900; sacred-texts.com

Hope, Murry; *The Sirius connection: Unlocking the Secrets of Ancient Egypt*; 1996; Element Books; Salisbury.

Horowitz, Wayne & Wasserman, Nathan; *Another Old Babylonian Prayer to the Gods of the Night*; 1996; in *Journal of Cuneiform Studies* Vol. 48:57-60.

Hulse, David Allen; *New Dimensions for the Cube of Space*; 2000; Weiser Books; Maine.

Hutton, Ronald; *Witches, Druids and King Arthur*; 2003; Hambledon Continuum; London.

----------; *The Druids: A History*; 2008; Hambledon Continuum; London.

Jackson, Howard M.; *Lion Becomes Man: The Gnostic Leontomorphic Creator and the Platonic Tradition* (Dissertation Series / Society of Biblical Literature);1985; Scholars Press.

Jackson, Nigel; *Celestial Magic: Principles and Practises of the Talismanic Art*; 2003; Capall Bann Publishing; Chievely.

Jong, Albert De; *Traditions of the Magi: Zoroastrianism in Greek and Latin Literature (Religions in the Graeco-Roman World)*; 1998; Brill Academic Publishers; Leiden.

Julian Cope; *Megalithic European: The 21st Century Traveller in Prehistoric Europe*; 2004; Element Books; Salisbury.

Kaplan, Aryeh; *Sefer Yetzirah: The Book of Creation: In Theory and Practice;* 1990; Red Wheel Weiser; Maine.

Kelley, David H., & Milone, Eugene F.; *Exploring Ancient Skies: An Encyclopedic Survey of Archaeoastronomy*; 2004; Springer; USA.

Lambert, W.G.; *Babylonian Astrological Omens and Their Stars*; 1987; in *Journal of the American Oriental Society*, Vol. 107:1:93-96.

Lewisohn, Leonard; *Classical Persian Sufism from Its Origins to Rumi*; 1993; Khaniqahi-Nimatullahi Publications; New York.

Marciniak, Barbara; *The Family of Light: Pleiadian Tales and Lessons in Living*; 1998; Bear & Company; Vermot.

Matthews, John & Caitlin; *Walkers Between Worlds: The Western Tradition from Shaman to Magus*; 2003; Inner Traditions; Vermont.

McGrath, Sheena; *Sun, Moon & Stars*; 2005; Capall Bann; Chievely.

Meyer, Marvin W.; *Ancient Mysteries: Sacred Texts of the Mystery Religions of the Ancient Mediterranean World*; 1999; University of Pennsylvania Press; Pennsylvania.

Michell, John; *A Little History of Astro-archaeology: Stages in the Transformation of a Heresy*; 1989; Thames & Hudson Ltd; London.

Morgan, Mogg; *Tankhem: Meditations on Seth Magick*; 2003; Mandrake of Oxford; Oxford.

----------; *Supernatural Assault in Ancient Egypt: Seth, Renpet and Moon Magick*; 2008; Mandrake of Oxford; Oxford.

----------; *The Bull of Ombos: Seth and Egyptian Magick II*; 2005; Mandrake of Oxford; Oxford.

Nabarz, Payam; *The Mysteries of Mithras: The Pagan Belief That Shaped the Christian World*; 2005; Inner Traditions; Vermont.

Nabarz, Payam & Taqizadeh, S.H.; *Persian 'Mar Nameh', The Zoroastrian 'Book of the Snake' Omens and Calendar & The Old Persian Calendar*; 2006; Twin Serpents Ltd; Oxford.

Nurbakhsh, Javad; *The Path: Sufi Practices*; 2002; Khaniqahi-Nimatullahi Publications; New York.

Ovid, & Innes, May M. (trans); *The Metamorphoses of Ovid*; 2002; Penguin Classics; London.

Ovid, & Riley, Henry Thomas (trans); *The Metamorphoses of Ovid Vol. I, Books I-VII*; 1893; gutenberg.org

Ovid, & Dryden, John; *Metamorphoses*; 1717, sacred-texts.com

Pingree, David; *Some of the Sources of the Ghāyat al-hakīm*; 1980; in *Journal of the Warburg and Courtauld Institutes* Vol. 43:1-15.

Plato, & Jowett, Benjamin (trans); *Timaeus*; 1871; C. Scribner's Sons; New York

Porphyry, & Taylor, Thomas (trans); *On the Cave of the Nymphs*; 1823; in the Thirteenth Book of the *Odyssey*; http://www.tertullian.org/fathers/porphyry_cave_of_nymphs_02_translation.htm

Pratt, John P.; *The Lion and Unicorn Testify of Christ Part II: The Four Royal Stars*; 2001; in Meridian Magazine Dec.5; www.meridianmagazine.com/sci_rel/011205royal.html.

----------; *The Lion and Unicorn Testify of Christ Part I: The Cornerstone Constellations;* 2001; Meridian Magazine, Nov. 8; www.meridianmagazine.com/sci_rel/011108lion.html

Price, Simon, & Kearns, Emily; *The Oxford Dictionary of Classical Myth & Religion*; 2003; Oxford University Press; Oxford.

Quan-Yin, Amorah; *The Pleiadian Workbook: Awakening Your Divine Karma;* 1995; Bear & Company; Vermont.

Rankine, David, & D'Este, Sorita; *Practical Planetary Magick: Working the Magick of the Classical Planets in the Western Mystery Tradition;* 2007; Avalonia; London.

Regardie, Israel; *A Garden of Pomegranates, Skrying on the Tree of Life*; 1999; Llewellyn Publications; Minnesota.

Reiner, Erica; *Astral Magic in Babylonia*; 1995; in *Transactions of the American Philosophical Society* Vol. 85.4:i-150.

----------; *The Uses of Astrology*; 1985; in *Journal of the American Oriental Society* Vol. 105.4:589-595.

Rigakis, Evangelos; *Threskia: Tradition of the Greek Mysteries*; 2002; Mandrake of Oxford; Oxford.

Roberts, Paul William; *Journey of The Magi: Travels in Search of the Birth of Jesus*; 2006; Tauris Parke Paperbacks; London.

Rock, Mike; *Picatrix Ghayat al Hakim or The Goal of the Wise*; http://picatrix.mike-rock.com/book3/p3ch3.php, 2007.

Schaefer, Bradley E.; *The Origin of the Greek Constellations*; 2006; in *Scientific American*, Nov:70-75.

Scully, Nicki; *Power Animal Meditations: Shamanic Journeys with Your Spirit Allies*; 2001; Bear & Company; Vermont.

Shah, Idries; *Oriental Magic*; 1993; Octagon Press, Limited; London.

Spat, Eszter; *The Yezidis*; 2005; Saqi.

Speidel, Michael P.; *Mithras-Orion: Greek Hero and Roman Army God*; 1980; Brill; Leiden.

Staal, Julius D.W.; *The New Patterns in the Sky: Myths and Legends of the Stars*; 1988; McDonald & Woodward Publishing Company; Ohio.

Stanley, Thomas (trans, ed); *The Chaldean Oracles of Zoroaster*; 1661; Thomas Dring; London; http://www.esotericarchives.com/oracle/oraclesj.htm

Tacitus, & Church, Alfred John (trans) & Brodribb, William Jackson (trans); *The Annals, The Complete Works of Tacitus;* 1942; sacred-texts.com.

Taylor, Thomas (trans); *The Hymns of Orpheus*; 1792, sacred-texts.com.

Temple, Robert K.G.; *The Sirius Mystery: Conclusive New Evidence of Alien Influence on the Origins of Humankind in the Traditions of an African Tribe*; 1998; Century; London.

Tester, Jim; *A History of Western Astrology*; 1996; Boydell Press; New York.

Townley, Kevin; *The Cube of Space*; 1993; Archive Press & Communications.

Warnock, Christopher; *Picatrix Ghayat al Hakim or The Goal of the Wise*, http://www.renaissanceastrology.com/picatrix.html, 2007.

West, E.W. (trans); *Pahlavi Texts, Part I Sacred Books of the East, Vol. 5*; 1880, sacred-texts.com

Westcott, W.W (trans); *The Chaldean Oracles Attributed to Zoroaster*, 1984; Sure Fire Press.

Woolley, Benjamin; *The Queen's Conjuror: The Science and Magic of Dr. Dee;* 2001; Harper Collins Publishers Ltd; London.

Zaehner, R.C.; *The Dawn and Twilight of Zoroastrianism*; 1961; G.P. Putnams Sons; New York.

Useful web resources:

- www.skyatnightmagazine.com

- http://hubblesite.org/explore_astronomy/tonights_sky

- Dictionary of Greek and Roman Biography and Mythology, page 1 (v. 1) http://www.ancientlibrary.com/smith-bio/0010.html

- Farmers' Almanac - Dates and Times of Full Moons
  http://www.farmersalmanac.com/astronomy/fullmoons.html

- Sun Signs in the Zodiac Astrology Information
  http://www.astrology-online.com/persn.htm

- The Chaldean Oracles of Zoroaster
  http://www.esotericarchives.com/oracle/oraclez.htm

- The Chaldean Oracles of Zoroaster Index
  http://www.sacred-texts.com/eso/coz/index.htm

- SILVERSTAR ezine
  http://www.horusmaat.com/silverstar

- Stellarium
  http://www.stellarium.org/screenshots.html

- The book Picatrix
  http://www.mike-rock.com/picatrix

- Picatrix (The Aim of the Sage) of pseudo-Majriti (summary)
  http://www.esotericarchives.com/picatrix.htm

- Cicero's Dream - Cicero - Somnium Scipionis - Dream of Scipio
  http://ancienthistory.about.com/library/bl/bl_text_cic_scipiodream.htm

- The Astrological Memory Theatre
  http://www.atmann.net/AstroMem1.htm

- The Sepher Yetsira (Sefer Yetzirah): Cube of Space: Physical and Psychological Faces
  http://www.psyche.com/psyche/cube/cube_ppfaces.html

- Offers maps and satellite images for complex or pinpointed regional searches.
  www.earth.google.com

- HubbleSite - Image: Hubble's Sharpest View of the Orion Nebula
  http://hubblesite.org/gallery/album/entire_collection/pr2006001a

INDEX

Ahriman.................... 101, 159
Ahura Mazda 65, 66, 67, 68, 69, 95, 96, 97, 101, 156, 159
Aion 159
Aldebaran 30, 32, 33, 35, 37, 172
Altair................................ 112
Ammon 172
Anahita..................... 82, 156
Andromeda 72, 73, 74, 76, 77, 78, 79, 193
Antares 31, 32, 33, 35, 37, 174
Aphrodite.......................... 82
Apollo ...45, 61, 111, 175, 188
Aquarius 31, 32, 33, 34, 39, 88, 166, 168, 174, 175, 192, 193
Aquila 34, 112
Arcturus 132, 143
Argo 46
Arianrhod 82, 85
Artemis 44, 45, 81, 82
Astarte 82
Astraea 173, 174
Athena 159
Atlas 45, 46, 62, 72, 111, 131, 132, 160, 163
Atum........................... 55, 186
Aurora 178, 179, 181, 182, 183
Bacchus........................... 106
Bellona 64
Beltane 30, 72, 74, 158
Betelgeuse.................. 50, 60
Bride................................ 82

Brigid 114
Cancer 87, 100, 166, 167, 173, 175, 187, 192
Canis Major 60, 61, 62, 63, 193
Canis Minor.......... 17, 60, 131
Canopus........................... 46
Capricorn 88, 101, 166, 168, 174, 175, 187, 192
Cassiopeia 72, 79, 193
Castor 144, 172
Cautes........................ 17, 191
Cautopates 17, 191
Cepheus 72, 73, 78, 79, 128, 193
Ceres 64, 106, 175, 188
Ceridwen 82, 83
Cetus..................... 72, 73, 79
Chandra 81
Cherubim 33, 34, 195
Corvus....................... 17, 131
Cupid 175
Cygnus 111, 112, 115, 121, 124, 125, 126, 128, 193
Damballah...................... 159
Debhe............................. 143
Demeter.............. 59, 132, 173
Deneb...................... 112, 121
Diana 45, 60, 64, 81, 82, 94, 107, 131, 149, 150, 175
Dike 173, 174
Dione............................... 82
Dionysus 132, 173
Draco 26, 35, 45, 115, 142, 143, 155, 156, 159, 161, 162, 163, 189, 193
Drvâspa...................... 156

Edfu 47, 48, 49, 54, 55, 56
Enkidu 47
Eos 179
Fomalhaut 31, 32, 33, 35, 39, 175
Friedswide 114
Gaia 45, 174
Geb 52, 53
Gemini 31, 87, 144, 166, 167, 172, 173, 175, 192
Gilgamesh 46
Giza 15, 45, 46
Great Bear 18, 26, 32, 141, 142, 143, 146, 147, 148, 149, 152, 193
Hades 173
Hathor 28, 46, 49, 133
Hecate 64
Helios 111, 126
Hephaestus 173
Hera 159, 172, 173
Hermes 46, 78, 104, 170
Horus 43, 46, 47, 48, 49, 50, 51, 52, 53, 54, 55, 178, 181, 186
Hyades 132, 172
Hydra 17, 131
Imbolc 31
Ishtar 173
Isis 46, 52, 53, 59, 64, 114, 116, 118, 119, 121, 133, 134, 173
Jove .... See Jupiter
Juno 33, 64, 146, 150, 151, 152, 160, 175
Jupiter 12, 16, 19, 33, 45, 100, 101, 102, 103, 104, 106, 112, 127, 131, 146, 174, 175, 179, 180, 192
Kheperi 173
Lammas 31

Leo 16, 19, 31, 32, 33, 34, 37, 46, 87, 143, 166, 167, 170, 173, 175, 192, 193
Leto 45
Libra 88, 166, 167, 170, 174, 175, 192
Little Bear 35, 141, 142, 143, 146, 147, 149, 152, 159, 189, 193
Luna 81
Lyra 26, 112, 128
Mah 81, 93, 95, 96
Mani 81
Marduk 156
Mars 16, 19, 26, 33, 100, 101, 102, 103, 104, 105, 168, 174, 175, 192
Medusa 73, 75, 77, 78
Melusine 82
Men 81
Merak 143
Mercury 16, 19, 45, 100, 101, 102, 103, 104, 168, 175, 192
Milky Way 17, 19, 46, 63, 79, 103, 113, 121, 128, 131, 174, 187
Min 49
Minerva 64, 175
Mithra 16, 61, 65, 68, 119, 165, 179, 192
Mithraeum 16, 18, 187, 191
Mithras 16, 17, 19, 21, 28, 44, 47, 59, 100, 131, 142, 165, 172, 178, 186, 187, 192
Moon 11, 12, 13, 14, 16, 18, 19, 31, 37, 40, 43, 64, 81, 82, 83, 84, 85, 86, 87, 88, 92, 93, 94, 95, 96, 97, 100, 102, 103, 104, 106, 114,

116, 137, 138, 143, 150, 158, 171, 179, 187, 192
Nefertem 52
Neptune 44, 175
Ninurta 60
Nuit 15, 52, 72, 76, 84, 85, 128, 133, 134, 178
Oceanus 133, 146
Ophiuchus 31, 37
Orion 26, 43, 44, 45, 46, 49, 50, 51, 52, 53, 55, 60, 63, 131, 132, 133, 138, 156, 174, 193
Ormazd 95
Osiris 28, 46, 52, 53, 82, 134, 186
Pales 100, 103
Pallas 78
Pan 174
Pegasus 72, 73, 79, 128
Persephone 173
Perseus 17, 72, 73, 74, 75, 76, 77, 78, 79, 131, 189, 193
Pisces 31, 39, 88, 166, 168, 175, 192
Pisces Australis 31, 39
Pleiades 17, 26, 44, 45, 46, 49, 114, 131, 132, 133, 134, 135, 137, 139, 142, 172, 179, 193
Plough .... See Great Bear
Polaris 143
Pole Star 35, 159, 189
Polestar 147
Pollux 144, 172
Poseidon 73, 172
Procyon 60, 61
Proserpina 64, 165
Ra 52, 53, 55, 179, 186
Regulus 31, 32, 33, 35, 37, 173

Rhea 108
Royal Stars 30, 32, 33, 34, 35, 36, 39, 187
Sagittarius 31, 44, 88, 166, 168, 174, 175, 192
Samhain 31, 85
Saturn 16, 19, 100, 101, 102, 103, 104, 108, 111, 188, 192
Scorpio 17, 31, 32, 33, 34, 37, 44, 45, 88, 112, 131, 166, 168, 174, 175, 192, 193
Selene 81, 93, 95
Seth 53, 143, 186
Seven Hathors 46, 49, 143
Shamash 174
Shiva 119, 156, 189, 195
Shu 53, 55
Sin 81
Sirius 26, 32, 45, 46, 59, 60, 61, 62, 63, 64, 70, 132
Sothis .... See Sirius
Spica 17, 131, 143, 173
Spring Equinox 88, 172
Star 59
Sun 11, 12, 13, 14, 16, 17, 18, 19, 31, 37, 40, 44, 45, 61, 63, 85, 100, 101, 102, 103, 104, 107, 111, 119, 132, 133, 134, 144, 149, 158, 165, 166, 168, 171, 173, 174, 175, 178, 179, 180, 181, 182, 188, 191, 192
Tammuz 173
Tauroctony 16, 17, 47
Taurus 17, 30, 32, 33, 34, 37, 44, 46, 87, 131, 166, 167, 172, 174, 175, 192, 193
Tefnut 53

Tethys............... 126, 146, 152
Thebes........................ 45, 172
Thoth................ 52, 53, 55, 81
Tiamat 156
Tir..................... 59, 60, 61, 64
Tishtrya 59, 60, 64, 65, 66, 67, 68, 69
Tsukiyomi.......................... 81
Typhon 46, 155, 159, 174, 175
Vega................................. 112
Venus 16, 19, 33, 64, 100, 101, 102, 103, 104, 106, 168, 175, 192

Vesta 175
Virgo 17, 31, 88, 131, 143, 166, 167, 173, 174, 175, 192
Vishnu 156
Yggdrasil 159, 189, 195
Zeus 45, 72, 95, 112, 113, 142, 159, 172, 173, 175
Zizaubio 134, 137
Zodiac 11, 28, 86, 112, 127, 159, 165, 166, 167, 168, 169, 170, 175, 192, 193, 194
Zurvan 159

Lightning Source UK Ltd.
Milton Keynes UK
172123UK00004B/35/P